Physical Best
ACTIVITY GUIDE
Secondary Level

American Alliance
for Health, Physical Education,
Recreation and Dance

American Alliance for
Health, Physical Education,
Recreation and Dance

Human Kinetics

Library of Congress Cataloging-in-Publication Data

Physical Best (Program)
    Physical Best activity guide—secondary level / American
Alliance for Health, Physical Education, Recreation and Dance.
      p.   cm.
    Includes bibliographical references.
    ISBN 0-88011-971-3
    1. Physical education and training--Study and teaching
(Secondary)--United States.   I. American Alliance for Health,
Physical Education, Recreation and Dance.   II. Title.
GV365.P4993   1999
613.7'043--dc21

                           98-40311
                           CIP

ISBN: 0-88011-971-3

Acquisitions Editor: Scott Wikgren; **Developmental Editor:** C.E. Petit, JD; **Assistant Editor:** Phil Natividad; **Copyeditor:** Denelle Eknes; **Proofreader:** Erin Cler; **Graphic Designer:** Nancy Rasmus; **Graphic Artist:** Kathleen Boudreau-Fuoss; **Photo Editor:** Boyd LaFoon, **Cover Designer:** Jack Davis; **Photographer (cover):** Tom Roberts; **Photographer (interior):** Tom Roberts, except where otherwise noted; **Illustrators:** (medical art) Beth Young, (line art) Roberto Sabas, and (Mac art) Kim Maxey; **Printer:** United Graphics

Printed in the United States of America   10 9 8 7 6 5 4

Human Kinetics
Web site: www.HumanKinetics.com

United States: Human Kinetics, P.O. Box 5076, Champaign, IL 61825-5076
800-747-4457
e-mail: humank@hkusa.com

Canada: Human Kinetics, 475 Devonshire Road, Unit 100, Windsor, ON N8Y 2L5
800-465-7301 (in Canada only)
e-mail: orders@hkcanada.com

Europe: Human Kinetics, 107 Bradford Road, Stanningley
Leeds LS28 6AT, United Kingdom
+44 (0) 113 255 5665
e-mail: hk@hkeurope.com

Australia: Human Kinetics, 57A Price Avenue, Lower Mitcham, South Australia 5062
08 8277 1555
e-mail: liahka@senet.com.au

New Zealand: Human Kinetics, P.O. Box 105-231, Auckland Central
09-523-3462
e-mail: hkp@ihug.co.nz

Contents _____

About Physical Best

Physical Best is the health-related fitness education component of a comprehensive physical education program. Additional program resources include:

- *Physical Best Activity Guide—Elementary Level*
- The companion teacher's guide, *Physical Education for Lifelong Fitness*
- *FITNESSGRAM* test for evaluating students' physical fitness, developed by the Cooper Institute for Aerobics Research (CIAR)
- Brockport Physical Fitness Test (developed specifically for students with disabilities)
- Educational workshops for teachers available through AAHPERD, which enable teachers to become certified as health-related physical education specialists, call 1-800-213-7193, extension 426

The Physical Best program is offered through The American Fitness Alliance (AFA), a collaborative effort of AAHPERD, CIAR, and Human Kinetics.

Acknowledgments

AAHPERD gratefully acknowledges the contributions of the following teachers to the *Physical Best Activity Guides*: Ellen Abbadessa (Arizona), Carolyn Masterson (New Jersey), Aleita Hass-Holcombe (Oregon), Jennifer Reeves (Arizona), Marian Franck (Pennsylvania), John Kading (Wisconsin), Suzann Schiemer (Pennsylvania), Ron Feingold (New York), W. Larry Bruce (Cuba), Barbara Cusimano (Oregon), Deborah Loper (Nebraska), Laura Borsdorf (Pennsylvania), Jeff Carpenter (Washington), Larry Cain (Wisconsin), Nancy Raso-Eklund (Wyoming), Kathleen Thorton (Maryland), Nannette Wolford (Missouri), and Lawrence Rohner (New Mexico).

AAHPERD would also like to thank the late Dr. Paul Saltman of the University of California at San Diego for his guidance on nutrition issues, and Gopher Sport and Mars, Incorporated for their financial support of the Physical Best program.

Special thanks to Anne Cahill for her invaluable contributions to the content and to Linda Thompson-Fuller and Jennie Gilbert Hartman for their assistance in coordinating this effort.

Preface

**"I hear and I forget. I see and I remember.
I do and I understand."—Chinese proverb**

Welcome to the *Physical Best Activity Guide—Secondary Level*. The activities we are sharing in this book have been designed and successfully used by physical educators from around the country to help their students "do and understand." They are designed to help students gain the the knowledge, skills, appreciation, and confidence needed to lead physically active, healthy lives and are part of Physical Best.

Physical Best is the health-related fitness education component of a comprehensive physical education program. It complements and supports—not necessarily replaces—existing physical education curriculums, and helps teachers assist students in meeting the NASPE National Physical Education Standards related to health-related fitness as well as the national standards in health, dance, and adapted physical education that relate to health-related fitness.

All Physical Best materials, resources, and workshops will:

- Emphasize enjoyable participation in physical activities that are relevant to students.
- Offer a diverse range of noncompetitive and competitive activities appropriate for different ages and abilities, allowing all students to successfully participate.
- Emphasize the personal nature of participation in lifelong physical activity.
- Provide appropriate and authentic assessment as part of the learning process, designed so students take on increasing responsibility for their own assessment.
- Follow proven educational progressions that lead to students taking increasing responsibility for their own health-related fitness.
- Enable students to meet the NASPE National Physical Education Standards for health-related fitness.

The History of Physical Best

In 1987 the American Alliance for Health, Physical Education, Recreation and Dance (AAHPERD) challenged the nation's youth to become more physically fit. One path to achieving this objective involved tapping our own resources, our physical educators. Physical Best was envisioned as a program to enhance an existing curriculum, supplement daily plans, or act as a total health-related fitness education package.

Physical Best is a total health-related fitness education curriculum package designed to assist youths in understanding the importance of a lifetime of physical activity. Yet this total package can be geared up or down for your school's particular needs/demands.

This program does not cater to the 10% or so who are athletically talented, but focuses on educating *all* students, regardless of their abilities, from a health-related viewpoint. Many health-minded organizations (including the American Academy of Pediatrics, American Medical Association, President's Council on Physical Fitness and Sports, the allied health community, and the U.S. Department of Health and Human Services) emphasize the importance of physical activity to our students. Even top athletes must understand the health aspects of lifelong physical activity so they do not become sedentary after completing their competitive athletic careers.

Based on these concepts, scholars and practitioners at AAHPERD developed Physical Best. First and foremost, Physical Best is educational. The elementary and secondary activity guides provide ideas for quick, easy activities and learning station ideas. You can easily include them in your existing plans or use them on their own. Through these activity guides and in combination with your own curriculum, you'll help your students understand why physical activity is important to their health.

Physical Best is individualized—students compete only with themselves, not against others. This philosophy complements that of the various practices of today's physical education textbooks. However, Physical Best differs from some in that it does not claim to stand alone, eliminating all other aspects of our discipline. The motivation, the test procedures, and the goal-setting program are all designed to work on self-improvement regardless of the student's level of skill and fitness. The *FITNESSGRAM* test battery is criterion-referenced. This inspires students to achieve personal goals, not strive to meet unrealistic standards, and to include physical activity in their lives outside of school. This Physical Best philosophy will remain the focus of the program as it expands and evolves.

Physical Best is a total health-related fitness education package. It is not designed as an instructional unit. It becomes a part of the "branching off" of other activities. It was designed so that instructors could use all or part of the package. It does not tie instructors down to day-to-day lesson plans. It encourages creativity and makes it easy for you to include elements of Physical Best in your existing program.

Inclusion in Health-Related Fitness

Everyone can benefit from a health-related fitness program, regardless of gender, culture, or ability. Inactivity and poor diet cause more preventable deaths each year in the United States than illicit use of drugs, firearms, sexual behavior, microbial agents, and alcohol *combined* (McGinnis and Foege 1993)! While not every student can equally benefit from, or even participate in, every activity, including everyone in your health-related fitness program isn't just a good idea—it's the law.

Including all of your students should not be an afterthought, but an important part of your planning and teaching process. We'll discuss some of the most significant inclusion issues in sidebars like this one throughout part I of this *Activity Guide*. We've also designed the activities for easy adaptation to a wide variety of special circumstances.

Physical Best Activity Guides

The *Physical Best Activity Guides* will help you bring the theory behind health-related fitness into your school with a variety of fun, developmentally appropriate activities that combine physical activity with other aspects of learning. Each

Activity Guide begins with a review of the health and teaching principles behind an effective health-related fitness curriculum. The *Activity Guides* then present a variety of activities that focus on the four elements of health-related fitness: aerobic fitness, muscular strength and endurance, flexibility, and body composition. These activities emphasize class management, keep group instruction and demonstration to a minimum, maximize the number of practice trials, and provide frequent individual feedback, instruction, and encouragement.

The *Activity Guides* are designed to facilitate a health-related fitness program at your school. You'll find further information in *Physical Education for Lifelong Fitness: The Physical Best Teacher's Guide.* This book provides a strong theoretical background for health-related fitness programs, including specific advice on integrating The Cooper Institute's *FITNESSGRAM* into a complete program. We're developing other Physical Best resources, including workshops with certification from AAHPERD.

We should be teaching our students what they need to know to become healthier. This can be accomplished by incorporating Physical Best into our existing lesson plans. Therefore, we can teach students how to become fit for life through fun, basic skill development and participation. Physical Best can help accomplish this goal via its developmentally appropriate activities and concepts. Let's put the education back into physical fitness education. Join us in using the new Physical Best.

PART I

Teaching Health-Related Fitness

Chapter 1

Health-Related Fitness

Fitness is defined as a condition in which an individual has sufficient energy to avoid fatigue and enjoy life. It is also defined as the capacity of the lungs and muscles to function at optimum efficiency (Pate 1983). The content area of physical fitness includes learning experiences associated with achieving optimum health through its four components.

Physical fitness can be divided into health- and skill-related components. Health-related fitness focuses on factors that promote optimum health and prevent the onset of disease and problems associated with inactivity. Health-related fitness includes cardiorespiratory (aerobic) fitness, muscular strength and endurance, flexibility, and body composition. Skill-related fitness includes balance, agility, coordination, power, reaction time, and speed. To help children develop active lifestyles, health- and skill-related fitness must be taught equally.

The components of health-related fitness can be measured separately, and exercises have been designed to improve each specific component. The most important point in physical education is to teach *total fitness* in ways that develop each of the areas of health-related fitness. Research demonstrates that individuals who engage in regular physical activities to improve the four components of health-related fitness increase their basic energy levels and lower their risk for heart disease, cancer, diabetes, osteoporosis, and other chronic diseases.

Components of Health-Related Fitness

A health-related fitness curriculum integrates physical fitness testing and education. A good physical-fitness curriculum emphasizes the four components of the health-related fitness: cardiovascular endurance, muscular strength and endurance, flexibility, and body composition (CDC 1999).

Cardiorespiratory Fitness

Cardiorespiratory endurance involves the ability of the heart and lungs to supply oxygen to the working muscles for an extended period of time. Also called aerobic endurance or fitness, it is the ability of the circulatory and respiratory systems to adjust to and recover from the effects of moderate to vigorous activity, such as brisk walking, running, swimming, or biking. Cardiorespiratory endurance is defined by a concept called maximum oxygen uptake ($\dot{V}O_2$ max)—in other words, how well one consumes oxygen during moderate-to-vigorous physical activity.

There are four techniques to help students improve their cardiovascular endurance: continuous, interval, Fartlek, and circuit-course activity. Continuous activity may include both aerobic and anaerobic activities. *Aerobic* activities, meaning "with oxygen," are done continuously, are of moderate intensity, and can be sustained over a period of time. *Anaerobic* activities are short blasts of activity done in the "absence of oxygen." Interval activity includes physical activity that alternates in intensity levels. Fartlek is similar to interval activity, but with it the terrain (such as hills) controls the intensity levels. Circuit training (circuit-course activity) combines continuous activity with flexibility and muscular strength-endurance activities, providing more variety.

Muscular Strength and Endurance

Muscular strength is a measure of the greatest force that can be produced by a muscle or group of muscles. *Dynamic strength* is the force exerted by a muscle group as the body moves, such as in a push-up. *Static strength* is the force exerted against an immovable object, such as pushing against a wall. The benefits of increasing muscular strength include a reduced risk of injury as well as improved posture, physical performance, and body composition. Developing strength requires working against a resistance in a progressive manner. Muscular strength can be improved in children, although they are incapable of producing large muscle masses.

Muscular endurance is the ability to contract a muscle or group of muscles repeatedly without incurring fatigue. The longer a muscle is used, the greater its endurance becomes. Locomotor activities help develop muscle endurance. The primary objective of developing muscular endurance in students is to enable participation in activity for longer periods of time before feeling muscle fatigue.

Basic guidelines have been established for resistance training and exercise progression in children (see Fleck and Kraemer 1997). Middle school students (ages 11 to 13) should learn all basic weight- and resistance-training techniques and engage in limited progressive loading. Instructors should emphasize proper technique, and may begin introducing more advanced exercises with little or no resistance. High school students should continue learning advanced exercises, including sport-specific exercises, while increasing exercise frequency. Instructors should continue to emphasize proper technique. As older students master techniques, they can begin participating in appropriate adult programs (Baechle and Groves 1998, 1994).

Flexibility

Flexibility is the ability of a joint to move freely in every direction or, more specifically, through a full and normal range of motion. Several factors can limit joint mobility, including genetic inheritance, the joint's structure, the amount of fatty tissue around the joint, and the body's temperature. Flexibility can be improved, however, with stretching.

The two most common types of stretching for primary and intermediate level children are static and ballistic stretching. *Static stretching* involves slow, gradual, and controlled elongation through a full range of motion. *Ballistic stretching* employs rapid, uncontrolled, and bouncing or bobbing motions. Ballistic technique is **not recommended** for the general population whose control may be compromised and whose risk of injury may be increased.

Body Composition

Body composition refers to the quality or makeup of total body mass. *Total body mass* is composed of lean body mass and fat mass. Lean body mass includes a person's bones, muscles, organs, and water. Fat mass is fat, adipose tissue. The assessment of body composition determines the relative percentages of the individual's lean body mass and fat mass. The skinfold caliper test is the most accurate method for measuring body composition generally available to teachers, if they are trained to use them.

Principles of FITT

The Physical Best program follows the FITT principles for improving and maintaining physical fitness. The principles of frequency (F), intensity (I), time (T), and type (T), along with overload and progression, are taught in each health-related concept. We outline them in this section.

Frequency

Frequency refers to the number of times a person engages in physical activity that is moderate to vigorous in nature. The prescribed frequency is related to the intensity and duration of the activity session. There are various standards as to how often one should exercise to improve or maintain physical fitness. According to the *U.S. Surgeon General's Report on Physical Activity and Health*, physical activity that is moderate to vigorous in nature should be done most days of the week.

Intensity

Intensity refers to the speed or workload used in a given exercise period. Intensity depends on the fitness goals of the exerciser and the type of training method being used. Aerobic intensity can be measured by checking one's heart rate. Middle school students should be able to monitor and record their own heart rates. High school students should also be able to make comparisons and draw conclusions from recorded heart rate data. Including a higher percentage of moderate-to-vigorous activities helps you match the needs of the students. Intensity with activities for muscular strength and endurance is the workload or resistance of the exercise. With flexibility, intensity is the range of motion the joint can achieve.

Intensity is directly related to how long one can sustain activity. Intensity is one of the hardest notions to teach, since pacing oneself is harder than going all-out. Intensity may have to be taught several times to instill safety precautions and to maximize the quality of the activity.

Time (Duration)

Duration refers to the number of minutes of physical activity. In cardiovascular endurance activities, duration is the amount of time spent doing the activity. Middle school students can safely engage in physical activity for 20 to 35 minutes at a time. High school students can safely engage in physical activity for 30 to 45 minutes at a time. When breaking between activities, students should rest for 2 to 3 minutes.

Time is how many repetitions and sets one performs in muscular strength and endurance activities. In flexibility exercise, on the other hand, time relates to how long a stretch is held before it is released. The recommended time for children to be physically active is 30 minutes most days of the week (CDC 1999).

Type (Specificity)

What type of exercise is selected is based on the principle of specificity. Specificity of training is the physiological adaptation to exercise that is specific to the system being worked or stressed during exercise. For example, the specific training exercises a youth does for flexibility do not increase his or her cardiovascular endurance.

Overload

Overload refers to increasing activity, frequency, intensity, or time to improve fitness levels. The body must perform harder than normal to improve. The overload principle is the basis for considering the variables of frequency, intensity, time, and type. To best explain overload to youths, let them experience it firsthand—through vigorous activity and by keeping track of how long they sustain activity or how many repetitions they perform.

Progression

Progression is *how* overload should take place. An increase in the level of exercise, whether it be to run farther or to add more resistance, must be done in a particular progression. This enables the body to adapt slowly to the overload; thus, it eventually makes the overload normal. Your students need to understand that improving their level of fitness is an ongoing process. To help them better understand progression and see that they are improving, give your students opportunities to track their progress. You can help them achieve this understanding effectively through pretests and posttests.

Fitness Is for Everyone

Physical activity, its assessment, and the opportunity to benefit from a health-related fitness education program are important to the well-being of all people in society, regardless of their gender, ethnicity, physical competence, or having particular disabilities. The concept of inclusion provides students with positive relationships through their interactions, and these interactions should carry the concepts through to adulthood. The overall mission of the physical educator is to help *all* students enjoy and learn about physical activity so that they will continue to be active the rest of their lives.

Individuals With Disabilities

Including individuals with disabilities in the physical education setting shows that physical activity is for everyone. It is the responsibility of every professional conducting physical activity programs to explore all options for including people with disabilities in their programs.

All people have equal rights to the health-related benefits of physical activity programs, and the values of these programs accrue equally to all. Participation in physical activity contributes to human growth and development. Emotional and social development flourishes through interaction with peers in play activities, but such opportunities often elude individuals with disabilities. By conducting properly planned and integrated programs, however, trained professionals can provide opportunities for people with disabilities to participate in developmentally appropriate activities.

As a professional conducting the program, the teacher is responsible for successfully including all participants. A leader shapes the attitudes of an entire group. Providing inclusive programs requires your gaining the necessary knowledge and skills to include individuals with disabilities, being accountable for a positive attitude, ensuring equal treatment across all lines of diversity, and effectively communicating, both verbally and nonverbally.

It is possible that regular physical education may not be an appropriate placement for some individuals with disabilities. Having support from parents, other teachers, a peer tutor, or a teacher assistant can sometimes alleviate disruptive behaviors (which often result in safety risks). However, if a student is not receiving any benefit from regular physical education, continues to be disruptive to others, or continues to pose a severe safety risk, an alternative placement is appropriate. Ongoing evaluation determines whether the alternative placement is effective for a particular student or whether participation in regular physical education one or more days a week would be more beneficial.

Students with disabilities shouldn't be placed in physical education classes solely for their social development or to have only passive roles, such as being a scorekeeper. The major purpose of participation in the physical education is to help students become active, efficient, and healthy movers. Physical education goals as defined by the IDEA, Part B, include development of gross motor skills, development of fundamental motor patterns, development of health-related fitness, and development of skills needed to participate in lifetime leisure pursuits, including individual and team sports.

Fitness for Individuals With Disabilities.   Fitness education and testing programs for individuals without special disabilities have traditionally emphasized a balanced approach, with expectations of achievement in all four physical fitness components. This approach represents the ideal—to maintain health-related standards of fitness in every way, including an active lifestyle.

Some individuals with disabilities, however, may have different lifestyles. For example, some may have great amounts of leisure time, others may have occupations demanding physical labor, still others, sedentary occupations or limited ambulating abilities. The health-related fitness profile for individuals with disabilities needs to be personalized according to disability, daily-living needs, current activities, and the person's potential.

Programming for Individuals With Disabilities.   To plan physical fitness activities that are appropriate for people with disabilities, you must consider the individual's initial or present level of performance. You can determine their present level of performance through a careful assessment of the person's physical fitness needs. The *Physical Best and Individuals with Disabilities Manual*, as well as other resources, provides tools for assessing the fitness level of someone with disabilities (*Adapted Physical Education National Standards*, NCPERID 1995).

Gender Inclusion

Physical education and sport are often gender-biased, which can perpetuate stereotypical beliefs and attitudes. Females, in general, have had fewer opportunities and less encouragement than males to be physically active. Physical activity is often more valued in the male domain. However, by eliminating systematic barriers and ensuring all individuals the freedom to develop their own interests and abilities, individuals, groups, and society all will benefit.

Gender-equitable education involves including the experiences, perceptions, and perspectives of girls as well as boys in all aspects of education. The inclusive strategies that promote girls' participating also reach boys, who are excluded from the girls' experiences, perceptions, and perspectives by more traditional styles of teaching and curricular content.

Physical educators, interacting daily with students, are in an ideal position to promote and affect desirable attitudinal changes in students. In providing a gender-equitable learning environment, you have opportunities to enhance students' sensitivity to gender considerations. Inequity can surface in the general physical education program, in access to resources such as equipment, and in the attention and interactions that teachers and coaches give or have with students. Equipment availability should reflect equal value placed on female and male participation. How educators and coaches organize for activity, assign responsibilities, and speak can either detract from or inspire gender sensitivity.

> ### Principles of Gender Equity in Education
> - All students have the right to a learning environment that is gender-equitable.
> - All education programs should be based on the students' abilities and interests.
> - Gender equity incorporates a consideration of social class, culture, ethnicity, religion, sexual orientation, and age.
> - Gender equity requires sensitivity, determination, commitment, and vigilance over time.
> - The foundation of gender equity is cooperation and collaboration among students, educators, educational organizations, families, and members of communities.

The National Association for Girls and Women in Sports has developed guidelines to ensure attention and interaction free of gender bias. These include the following:

- Distributing leadership and demonstration roles among all students
- Assigning nonstereotypical responsibilities to both genders
- Modifying game rules to involve all students, without losing the essence of the game, and explaining why modifications are desirable
- Handling behavior problems consistently among both females and males, not using gender-based assumptions as punishments
- Using nonsexist language
- Avoiding the use of gender as the sole criteria for grouping
- Not tolerating or allowing inequitable student-to-student interactions of a verbal or physical nature
- Incorporating several learning styles

Gender equity is important at all age levels. Educators should ensure that the student-to-student interactions are positive. Avoid making or tolerating negative statements, such as calling girls "sissy" or "tomboy." Language cues that are respectful and nonsexist should be the norm. Choosing females and males equally as leaders of groups and as demonstrators can help eliminate gender bias.

To promote gender equity, you can include activities that promote a wide movement repertoire for all students. You can provide students with curricular choices to ensure that assessments and intramural activities are not gender-biased.

Cultural Sensitivity

Cultural variables may significantly affect the delivery and learning of health information, and you should consider them when designing a physical education program. Although some similarities do exist within or between groups, differences do, too, and you should examine them for their potential impact on the design and implementation of a health education program.

Culture is learned and shared by a group of people. It teaches what to fear, what to respect, what to value, and what to regard as relevant in life. It encompasses many variables, including values, beliefs, and perceptions that given people exhibit. Cultural variables include the group of people in one's life who are considered to be family members and the relationships these people have to one another. Cultural variables do not include situational and environmental conditions. Culture is a continuous and cumulative process, rather, a continuum that individuals move along throughout their lives. Experiences over time contribute to movement along the continuum. Teachers, students, and families can be found at different points along their culture's continuum.

From culture to culture, the perception of physical activity will differ. In some cultures thinness is perceived to be a desirable health goal; in others, thin people may be considered in poor health, whereas fat people are thought to be healthy and happy. Natural body odors may be acceptable and desirable in some cultures, but offensive to others, especially in physical activity.

Bias in physical education instruction can affect students' self-images, philosophies of life, interpersonal sensitivities, opinions about different cultural groups, and opinions about social problems. Studies have shown that students who feel they are portrayed in stereotypical ways will internalize these notions and fail to develop their own unique abilities, interests, and full potentials. If teachers become aware of their own uncomfortable feelings, they may find it easier to recognize uncomfortable feelings among their students. Once teachers become comfortable with the differences, they can move on to create pleasant experiences that build comfort, acceptance, and respect for diversity in their students and others.

Effective communication with a student is the teacher's most powerful tool for overcoming cultural barriers. It is best that messages about physical activity and health not conflict with existing cultural beliefs, values, and perceptions. When appropriate, messages can acknowledge existing cultural practices, building on cultural strengths and pride.

Benefits of Fitness

Regular moderate physical activity results in many health benefits for adults. Physical activity has been proven in adults to decrease the risks of diseases that cause mortality and morbidity. Although more research is needed on the association of physical activity and health among young people, evidence already shows that physical activity brings some health benefits for children and adolescents. It improves aerobic endurance as well as muscular strength and endurance, and it decreases the risk factors that lead to cardiovascular disease. Physical activity among adolescents is consistently related to higher levels of self-esteem and self-concept and with lower levels of anxiety and stress.

Physical activity of course has direct benefits on a student's health. Physical activity

- makes the heart pump more strongly;
- helps lower blood pressure and resting heart rates;
- reduces the risks of heart disease;
- strengthens the bones and muscles;
- gives you more energy to do school work, daily chores, and play;
- helps maintain a healthy body weight; and
- reduces stress.

It is important to keep in step with the constant changes in our lives. Modern machines, computers, and other conveniences have made it possible to avoid physical activity. Substantial evidence links the adulthood problems of obesity, high blood pressure, and stroke to failure to develop a physical activity habit during childhood.

Process or Product?

The goal of teaching fitness to students is helping them acquire the skills, knowledge, and attitudes that lead to a lifetime of physical activity. Teaching fitness should be viewed as a long-term process of educating students about physical fitness and the importance of regular activity. The process starts out with achieving lower-order objectives, and it gradually moves to more complex, higher-order objectives that guide students toward valuing fitness and becoming self-directed. Corbin (1987) refers to this process as the "Stairway to Lifetime Fitness."

The Stairway to Lifetime Fitness is a description of hierarchical objectives for a fitness education program. Students move from a level of dependence to independence as they progress educationally through life. As students grow older, they move up each of the five steps toward lifetime fitness. The focus on a particular objective will change as the learner proceeds up the stairway.

Step 1:   *Doing regular exercise.* At this stage fitness scores are not important. Children learn what is fun and learn to love exercise. They will develop personal habits of doing exercise regularly.

Step 2:   *Achieving physical fitness.* Fitness is temporary. If children achieve fitness goals without obtaining a love for fitness, they will not maintain fitness for life.

Step 3:   *Personal exercise patterns.* At this level students learn what activities they personally enjoy doing and can make decisions about personal exercise patterns that are best for them. What is best for one child is not necessarily best for another. Educators begin to relinquish the decision-making process to the students. The role of the educator is to guide the students in making personal activity choices that are sound and realistic.

Step 4:   *Self-evaluation.* By this stage students realize what activities they enjoy the most. They begin to establish personal habits and patterns of lifetime exercise. To be fully educated, the older students must be able to assess their own fitness, having a basis for making informed decisions about lifetime fitness. By learning self-evaluation, they can revise their fitness programs as needed.

Step 5:   *Problem solving.* Students know the facts about each of the essential components of health-related fitness and are able to plan their own programs. The students essentially become informed consumers in fitness.

Corbin points out that it is the process of exercise that is important when teaching fitness education. If people can do the correct exercises for a lifetime (i.e., as a process) then the product (i.e., physical fitness) will follow. The objectives of teaching health-related fitness are met when the process becomes a regular, permanent part of a person's lifestyle.

Lifetime Implications for Health and Well-Being

There is little doubt that regular exercise is an important part of a healthy lifestyle. Most experts feel that children and youths need daily physical activity to keep fit and healthy. We have some information already about the effects of physical activity on improving the health of children and how it can carry over into adulthood. Researchers note that when children engage in physical activity, they mix very short bursts of intense activity with easy-to-moderate activity. Children have difficulty in exercising at one pace for 20 minutes or longer.

Most researchers have reported that the cardiorespiratory systems of children and youths respond to regular aerobic exercise in a way similar to adults. Dr. Thomas Rowland has shown that children can improve aerobic fitness after training, but that the increase is far less in youngsters than in adults. As a result of his findings, Dr. Rowland concluded that children often have high aerobic fitness levels to begin with, that adults may train more effectively than children, and that the bodies of children may lack the ability to adapt and respond fully to regular exercise (Rowland 1990).

Most studies suggest that obese children and youths are less physically active than their peers. Long-term inactivity on the part of children increases the likelihood of being overly fat. Students who are active and lean have less chance of being overly fat later in adulthood. Obesity among youths has been linked to other risk factors for disease, such as high blood pressure and cholesterol. Studies show that heart disease, cancer, and other chronic diseases are linked to the lifestyles of people and that these behaviors are learned in childhood and adolescence.

Physically inactive children and youths who begin to exercise regularly have lower resting blood pressures and more favorable blood-lipid profiles. In addition, body fat decreases when exercise programs are initiated among children. One of the most valuable health benefits in youth is that when vigorous activity occurs early in life, a higher bone-mineral density is achieved. Most bone buildup occurs during adolescence, so vigorous activity in the earlier years reduces the risk of osteoporosis later in life. Weight-bearing exercises are better for building stronger bones in children than are weight-supported exercises. All of the body's muscles should be exercised to build strong bones.

People begin to acquire and establish patterns of health-related behaviors during childhood and adolescence. Thus, we should encourage young people to engage in physical activity. Schools and communities can improve the health of students by providing instruction, programs, and services that promote enjoyable, lifelong physical activity (CDC 1999).

Chapter 2 ────────────────────

Physical Activity Behavior and Motivation

Over the past 20 years a lot has been learned about the various health benefits of regular activity. Recently, with the release of the *U.S. Surgeon General's Report on Physical Activity and Health*, research has demonstrated the health benefits of moderate-to-vigorous physical activity and, more important, the positive preventive health effects that activity has on adults and children. The task now is to promote healthful physical activity among the population. The important issue for promoting activity is to understand the reasons and behavioral changes underlying a person's level of activity.

Research on physical activity and behavior has examined what influences physical activity and what effect intervention programs have on the activity level of individuals. Half the adult population is mainly sedentary. The problem is how to get them active and, once they are active, how to keep them going. It is much easier for people to start an exercise program than to continue it on a regular basis. Adults cite as reasons for exercising achieving better weight control, reducing blood pressure, relieving stress and depression, finding enjoyment, increasing self-esteem, and improving their social life. Many people choose *not* to be active, despite the social, health, and personal benefits of exercising. The reasons these people cite for their inactivity are a lack of time, a lack of knowledge about fitness, inadequate facilities, and feelings of fatigue.

Personal, situational, behavioral, and programmatic factors determine whether someone adheres to a program of physical activity and exercise. These determinants influence both child and adult participation in physical activity. Studies have shown that influences while growing up also play a major role in the adherence to activity in adulthood.

Among the personal factors that influence and determine physical activity are an individual's exercise history, knowledge of or beliefs in health benefits, and personality. People who participate in sports and activity as youngsters have similar adherence patterns. Active youths who receive parental encouragement for physical activity will become more active adults than will the children who received no such encouragement. Studies show that high school and college experiences with sport increase the likelihood of exercise adherence in adulthood.

Knowing about the health benefits of physical activity is not enough, however, to inspire activity adherence. Some adults fail to adhere to exercise programs because of negative attitudes they acquired about physical activity when they were younger, and some adults are impeded by a lack of knowledge about the appropriate activity. It is important that knowledge about health-related fitness be an integral part of a fitness education program for adherence to occur later in life.

Self-motivation is consistently related to exercise behaviors and adherence. Individuals who are intrinsically motivated tend to adhere to exercise plans than those who rely on external reasons to exercise.

Situational factors can help or hinder regular participation in physical activity. Social support is critical to enhancing adherence rates among people in exercise programs. When youths participate in activities, they seek out approval from teachers, parents, and peers. Adults can also utilize positive social reinforcement. Time is the primary reason that adults give for not pursuing physical activity. Many sedentary people who lack motivation may rationalize that they lack time. It becomes an excuse for not exercising.

Sport psychologists have studied different techniques to enhance adherence to exercise. The different techniques they develop fall into five nonexclusive categories: environmental, reinforcement, goal setting and cognition, decision making, and social support. As environmental approaches they have used prompts, such as signs or bulletin boards for reinforcing the behavior. Having a choice of activities to choose from appears to promote adherence. Reinforcement techniques in exercise adherence must promote self-motivation. These techniques might include occasional rewards, positive feedback, and methods for self-monitoring. Goal-setting techniques should be self-set, rather than having an instructor set them; flexible, rather than fixed; and time-based, rather than distance-based. Using decision making to enhance adherence involves the participants in the program's structure. Social support, however, is the most important approach with children and adults who are participating in physical activity.

School physical education is probably the most important intervention for promoting students' physical activity and fitness. School physical education is only part of an overall effort to promote desirable physical activity patterns in youths. As in adults, other personal factors figure in the mix with students, such as biological and psychological influences. Gender is an important determinant in physical activity. From preschool through adolescence and often into adulthood, boys tend to be more active than girls (Sallis 1991). Positive trends among girls must be encouraged and accelerated to provide them with equal access to and support for healthful physical activity. The decline in physical activity participation is the steepest from childhood to adolescence, and it continues into adulthood.

Knowing *how* to be healthy and physically active is probably more important than knowing why (Desmond et al. 1986). Some knowledge may be helpful to start a student exercising, but it is rarely enough to keep a student active. The positive social and emotional effects of physical activity are powerful motivators for children, so they are what you should stress.

Social and physical environmental factors influence levels of physical activity not only in adults, but also in adolescents and teenagers. Social influence includes peer modeling and support. Peers are very important determinants of children's physical activity patterns. The physical environment is more important in determining physical activity levels outside the school, because physical education programs are usually designed for a particular local climate and the community's resources. Children and teenagers do most of their activity in the context of organized programs such as after-school programs, youth sports leagues, and clubs. When the goal of an organization is to promote *lifelong* physical activity among students, the levels of adherence to physical activity increase. Television and technology also affect children's activity levels.

All these factors are associated with physical activity levels, so effective intervention must operate at many levels. No single approach is likely to be effective. Children's needs change with age. Special attention should be devoted to girls and to adolescents since their activity levels are relatively low. But it is vital that physical education should prepare all students for a lifetime of physical activity, just as other teachers prepare them for a lifetime of learning and work. Physical education should teach students how to seek other avenues for physical activity and not rely solely on physical education classes.

Motivation

The importance of physical activity in a healthy lifestyle has been recognized for years. Data about the benefits of physical activity to children and youth are scarce. Debates continue, for example, about the extent to which youths and children are

The physical, intellectual, and emotional growth and development of middle and high school students make them very different from both elementary school children and adults. This must be considered when developing strategies to motivate them.

active, with some of the data's problems reflecting difficulties in measurement. What seems to be emerging, however, is that children's activity levels decline through the teenage years and that boys are more active than girls.

Whatever explanations account for a decrease in activity levels in children, it seems desirable to encourage children's activity for health and developmental reasons. Theorists and researchers have attempted to support determination to exercise but little is yet known about the possible determinants of physical activity in children. One explanation is given by *social-cognitive theory*. This approach to motivation in physical activity involves constructs of self-efficacy (self-perceptions of worth or competence) and, more recently, perceptions of success and definitions of achievement goals (Biddle and Goudas 1996).

Physical education must aim to maintain lifetime exercise (a process) rather than to improve short-term fitness (a product). Adults tend to talk mostly about the product of physical activity, whereas most youngsters discuss physical activity as a process. Youngsters emphasize being included in activities, being wanted by friends, and participating in "fun." In most cases, they learn to value fitness as an end product rather than an ongoing process. Sport psychologists know this "product" as extrinsic motivation.

Motivation takes two general forms: extrinsic and intrinsic. *Extrinsic motivation* involves factors outside the individual, unrelated to the task being performed (Ormrod 1995). Extrinsic motivators can be rewards that encourage participation, help children work to full potential, and recognize success. Although these extrinsic rewards do promote achieving activity goals to some extent, they also have numerous drawbacks. Students view the extrinsic rewards, which are used to control or manipulate them into participating, as the reason to participate in events, activities that they might otherwise have chosen to do on their own (Raffini 1993). In relation to physical activity, if a student participates in activity knowing there is a reward at the end, then he or she focuses solely on participating for the reward and not for personal satisfaction or accomplishment. Extrinsic rewards, thus, do not promote lifetime physical activity patterns. If teenagers are given extrinsic rewards they tend to focus on the product (the reward) instead of on the process, and they may stop working once the reward has been received. When they choose to participate on their own, however, and experience feelings of competence, then extrinsic rewards may help reinforce those feelings. This in turn enhances their intrinsic motivation to participate in physical activity. The key is to introduce extrinsic rewards in a correct manner at ideal times.

Intrinsic motivation is an individual's internal desire to perform a particular task (Ormrod 1995). Unlike extrinsic rewards, intrinsic motivations promote long-term behavioral changes more effectively. Students working in environments that emphasize intrinsic motivation tend to view physical activity as a process. This ongoing process can lead them to personal satisfaction and competence.

"Fun" is the primary reason, in terms of the experience of intrinsic pleasure, that students give for participating in physical activity. Fun, intrinsically motivating activities involve four characteristics: challenge, curiosity, control, and creativity (Raffini 1993). Teachers must empower students to develop the self-confidence to believe they can accomplish certain tasks, the self-esteem to believe they are worthy, and the self-efficacy to believe they are in control of their lives.

For years, students in physical education have been turned off by exercise. Consider why kids are in physical education: to increase physical activity, improve physical fitness, and improve fitness knowledge. To accomplish these goals and help them develop lifetime habits of physical activity, the key is choosing activities that follow the intrinsic feelings and perceptions kids have. Teachers should invoke students' curiosity. If the activity is too easy, kids may become bored. Some bored and frustrated learners may at times need extrinsic motivation to be convinced to exercise. Activities need to be developmentally appropriate for the level and include challenges to spark the curiosity.

As educators, give students a sense of control over the activities. Teach basic skills first. If you take the time to instruct students on the proper form and techniques, they can begin to master these basic skills. The more decisions the students then make in an activity, the more control they have. This type of control teaches them self-responsibility.

You must also provide activities that allow students to be creative about the content of the activity. This gives them a chance to use their creative thinking skills. It has the additional advantage of including students who are not as active or coordinated as well as the more naturally physically adept. By adding new, exciting equipment for classes, you can provide adventure and fun in students' activities. Decorating the gym with posters, charts, and bulletin boards creates a colorful environment—just like health clubs and even large corporations display motivational and informational posters.

Students need support and encouragement for their hard work in class. Occasionally provide positive, healthy incentives for active participation. Expressions of motivation are important as well. Some examples of words that connote or promote feelings of intrinsic motivation are *play, excitement, mastery, success, improvement,* and *freedom.* Phrases to encourage students may include *Great job! Way to go! Terrific! Very creative!* and *Much better!* Gestures also are important in encouraging intrinsic motivation. Giving the high five, nodding approvingly, shaking hands, and laughing with a student are all ways to encourage and enhance intrinsic motivation.

Parental support is considered one of the most important determinants of children's involvement in physical activity. Parents can influence their children by modeling physical activity behaviors. Biddle and Goudas (1996) showed clearly the importance of parent and teacher encouragement in strenuous physical activity. Parental encouragement created greater adherence to physical activity through increasing a sense of competence.

In theory and in practice, intrinsic motivation is the key to making physical activity a lifelong habit. A teacher's focus should be to help students internalize motivation and to create opportunities that can give them a sense of accomplishment from within. When intrinsic motivation for physical activity is present, the awards, prizes, and payments become immaterial. Physical education programs should strongly motivate children to maintain their own fitness. Here, in summary, are suggestions for motivating students:

1. Award the *process* of participation, rather than the *product* of fitness.
2. Set goals that are challenging yet attainable.
3. Use visual aids to publicize items of interest in fitness.
4. Emphasize self-testing programs that teach students to evaluate their own fitness levels.
5. Do not use fitness-test results for grading.
6. Involve the parents.

Working toward that happy state in which physical activity sparks the fun, thrill, and excitement in students to carry out continuing fitness activity for a lifetime should be a worthwhile goal for any teacher.

Goal Setting

According to the *U.S. Surgeon General's Report on Physical Activity and Health*, students should be physically active most days of the week by doing moderate to vigorous activity. The guidelines set by the American College of Sports Medicine recommend that a fitness class for any age be at least 20 minutes in length and meet at least three times a week. It takes good educational programs, caring instructors, time, facilities, and a desire to improve for students to feel motivated to engage in lifetime healthful behaviors. Most school systems do not allow enough time in physical education to make teaching health skills and fitness a priority for most students. Still, it is vital to encourage students to become active both inside *and* outside of the physical education classroom.

Foundations for Goal Setting

Attaining fitness benefits often requires several weeks of activity, depending on how frequently your class meets each week and the duration of each exercise period. Formal pre- and posttesting should not occur too soon or too often, although frequent and informal self-testing is helpful to monitor progress. A year-long program will not necessarily result in achieving twice as much fitness as a semester-long program, but fitness planning should be incorporated into the entire program. If you carefully followed all FITT variables, measurable fitness changes might be noted after only nine weeks of class; however, an entire semester (about 16 weeks) is a more realistic timeframe for inducing measurable fitness changes, provided the frequency and intensity have been adequate. A six- or nine-week retest is useful as a check on whether the initial goals were realistic. The retest or ongoing self-testing and informal testing results can be used to reset and fine-tune the final goals. Scores will naturally change as a student matures.

The rewards students look for are usually more extrinsic in nature than intrinsic. However, the intrinsic reward of self-improvement brings about behavioral changes that last for a much longer period of time. Goal setting is a mechanism that helps students understand their limits and feel satisfied with their accomplishments. Using goals created from personal assessments establishes their ownership and fosters pride in the process.

Behavior-modification programs are successful because goals are set and action plans are written to help meet those goals. Action plans help to establish a pathway to that destination. Allowing students to write goals based on their performances teaches them the importance of setting goals. They can apply this little teaching technique easily to other areas of their lives. The types of behaviors (goals) students require for improving health fitness can be determined from a pretest. Without goal setting, fitness scores are just data to submit to an administrator or to parents. By incorporating goal setting into the curriculum, fitness scores become much more meaningful. Establishing goals is a good way to encourage changes in behavior leading to improved health and fitness. Goal setting must be done carefully to successfully enhance motivation.

Goal setting takes experience and practice for both the students and educator. You must consider certain factors when setting goals with students. First, students' fitness levels vary widely. Girls and boys differ in certain fitness variables. Growth and maturation also influence fitness levels. The criteria-level charts provided in the *FITNESSGRAM* program reflect both gender and age differences. The teacher should be sure to use the proper charts when setting goals for each student.

The goals for each student should reflect the individual's level of fitness and fitness habits: greater magnitude of goal for less-fit students and lesser magnitude of goal for fitter students. A fit student will have to work hard to make small gains that bring him or her close to personal potential. A less-fit student, expending the same effort, might show dramatic fitness gains but still remain far below his or her potential. Focus not on comparisons between students but on personal improvement and progress toward personal goals.

Consider also a student's fitness habits. If a youngster has poor flexibility and is already taking part in activities that enhance flexibility in specific joints, then the goal should be set lower than if the same student with poor flexibility rarely does stretching activities. In the second situation, the fact that the student rarely does the appropriate activity opens the possibility that the student might respond well to stretching. In the first situation, on the other hand, where the student already stretches but remains at a low level of flexibility, factors other than exercise might be affecting that student's range of motion. Therefore, goals are always specific to an individual.

Identifying activity habits can also help you find what is likely to motivate a student to participate.

And with habits, remember that exercise is not the only factor contributing to fitness. Regularly consuming a proper diet, maintaining good sleep patterns, and controlling stress are also important. Discovering a student's habits in all these areas will improve your helping the child to individualize and set realistic goals.

Goal setting can be intimidating and time consuming if you are a teacher who has several large classes. Having successful strategies beforehand for teaching students goal setting will help you undertake the task.

Cultural Inclusion

It is important for physical education teachers to know about various cultures because all students are cultural beings. A culture encompasses many of the predisposing, enabling, and reinforcing factors affecting students' health behaviors and status. It affects health and activity decisions. As cultures vary, so do notions of what a human body symbolizes; how it should appear; how it functions most appropriately; and why, when, and how it should be treated. Responses about what is appropriate vary from culture to culture. Cultural values, beliefs, and perceptions influence students' abilities to understand, internalize, and exercise positive health practices that will enhance their quality of life. A culture can help solve problems and conflicts in the school and in the community, making it worth your while to become acquainted with such values. Giving a student messages that invalidate his or her cultural beliefs or values can damage a student's self-esteem. Goal setting should occur based on cultural beliefs. In some cultures, for example, competitive goals are unacceptable for girls, so individualizing goals is better.

Curricular content need not be different when the student population is culturally diverse. Activities that present challenge, risk taking, problem solving, and critical thinking are appropriate at the elementary level. Every student should be encouraged to accept various roles in all physical education activities, at the same time respecting cultural values. At the elementary level the curriculum can include movement education and guided discovery activities that pair words and concepts from several languages in movement tasks, creative dance, rhythmic activities, cooperative tumbling, games, and thematic play. Homework assignments might include studying the contributions to physical education and sport made by individuals (such as Olympians) from various cultures.

Students' ability to integrate their personal and cultural selves is a valuable skill for change. Modeling the integration of content about the contributions of various cultures is vital; it can demonstrate effective ways of using health information within the class.

Basic Strategies for Successful Goal Setting With Students

First, encourage students to set goals based on their current fitness status rather than on a comparison of their personal status with others'. Motivation is related to competence or perceptions of success in a particular area, so basing success on current physical fitness levels allows each student the potential to improve and thus experience success at goal setting. This positive experience will influence the student's motivation and behavior. Following several goal-setting guidelines will help motivate students maximally and positively influence their behavior and attitude toward physical activity.

Involve Students in the Goal-Setting Process.   Involving students enhances their commitment to achieving their goals and encourages self-responsibility for personal fitness. Scores should be their own, not norm-based. Consider the age, maturity level, and knowledge level of each student, which should influence the amount of input you use. And, of course, an individual's interests and needs should be part of establishing his or her fitness goals.

Start Small and Progress.   Start with a small class. Begin the goal-setting process with one grade level (e.g., 6th grade if you teach middle school or freshman if you teach high school) and continue to set goals with this class as its members progress through the school system. By 12th grade, they will be experienced in setting goals in all areas of fitness.

Focus on Improvements Relative to an Individual's Past Behavior.   Take into account the student's initial level of performance. The lower the level of performance, the greater the potential for improvement. The higher the level, the less improvement is possible. If a student has problems with motivation, set the individual's goals at lower increments than you might for a student who is already highly motivated. For example, you might need to cajole the less-motivated student more than you would others.

Set Specific and Measurable Goals.   Specific and measurable goals are more effective than vague goals (such as "I'll run faster"). For example, if a student wants to run faster and has already completed the mile in 9:40, you can help the student set a more specific, measurable goal of running the mile in 9:25. Students need some instruction, direction, and practice in identifying specific, measurable goals. If the goals are not measurable, it is impossible to determine if the student has been successful at achieving them, which defeats the purpose of goal setting.

Set Challenging and Realistic Goals.   When you assist students in setting physical fitness goals, take into consideration the child's initial fitness level. Also plan the time carefully between the pretest (to establish the goal) and the posttest (to measure the achievements). The lower the student's initial fitness level and the longer the time between testing periods, the greater his or her potential for improvement. The higher the student's initial fitness level and the shorter the time between testing periods to work on fitness, the less potential for improvement. It is important that the goal not be so easy that it does

Sample Goals for Aerobic Fitness

- I will reduce my mile run by ___ seconds by performing aerobic activity ___ times per week for at least ___ minutes each session.
- I will exercise aerobically ___ times a week, running the one-mile distance at least ___ times a week, timing and logging the results.
- I will perform aerobic activity ___ times a week, recording the amount of time, type of activity, and intensity of the activity.
- I will walk briskly ___ times a week for a total of ___ blocks. Each week I will increase my distance ____ blocks.

not challenge the student. Most students make their goals too difficult, and their motivation suffers when they cannot attain their goals. It may be helpful to have students practice setting goals and making intermediate goals until they learn more about themselves and their physical fitness levels.

Write Down Goals.   Written goals hold more meaning for students and help them focus on what they need to accomplish. If you work with poor readers or dyslexic students, it can help to use alternative methods such as pictures. The appendix contains a sample contract form for recording specific goals. These are masters that you can use or adapt to fit your program needs. You will also need to spend more time with students who have special health conditions. These students usually need extra guidance or incentives.

Provide Students With Strategies.   Students must understand *how* to change behaviors that are detrimental to improving or maintaining physical fitness. You can suggest examples of strategies, such as having them ride their bike three times a week, do 25 sit-ups each night before bed, or stretch after the day at school by using a series of stretches that you provide. In other words, provide strategies for improvement. It would be better, of course, if the students eventually develop strategies on their own with your guidance. Learning how to develop goals based on FITT and nutrition is a crucial part of the lifelong fitness process.

Support and Give Feedback About Progress Toward Goals.   An important aspect of goal setting that many teachers disregard is giving positive reinforcement and encouragement. Verbal encouragement (such as "I see you have been running one mile every other day. Keep up the good work!", written encouragement (such as a note: "John, I was glad to see you in-line skating in the park yesterday—that's a good aerobic workout"), and verbal recognition (such as "Susan has set a great example for all of us by doing her flexibility exercises daily!") can assist in keeping students committed to positive fitness behaviors.

Create Goal Stations.   Setting up "goal stations" for students helps instill a sense of ownership as the youngsters write their goals. The students can rotate in small groups to work on particular goals. You can group the students according to their receiving similar scores on their assessments. They will likely have similar goals and provide one another extra motivation and encouragement in achieving the goals. As they enter the class, students can also work individually at these stations to improve (instant activity). Allowing them to choose work areas places the responsibility for improvement on them.

Provide Opportunities for Periodic Assessment.   Periodic reassessment of fitness behavior helps students assess how they are progressing toward their personal goals. Assessment opportunities should occur regularly throughout the year. These reassessment opportunities can include informal testing and self-testing, both in school and at home. Use the information gained through reassessment to evaluate and adjust existing goals where necessary. You and the students will also have the opportunity after reassessments to change their goals and determine whether the goal was perhaps too difficult or too easy.

Building a Fitness Program Around Student Goals

The Physical Best program is a model for establishing goals in physical fitness levels, activity participation, and the affective and cognitive domains. The Physical

Best program recognizes the achievement of goals set by students, an important reinforcement for student motivation.

Using goal-setting techniques and strategies helps students have positive experiences through movement activities, feel good about themselves in physical activity, and carry positive fitness habits for a lifetime. Physical educators can support the students' use of goal setting to enhance their lives and fitness abilities.

Table 2.1 provides some guidelines for setting fitness goals, but the numbers in the chart are simply guidelines. The *FITNESSGRAM* package includes detailed criteria for each fitness component and testing regime. Initial level of fitness is already built into the table:

- Low—initial level is far from reaching the criteria levels
- Moderate—initial level is close to the criteria levels
- High—initial level is at or above the criteria levels

Nevertheless, each of the other unique circumstances each student presents must be considered for establishing that student's goals. For example, two moderately fit students might establish upper-body strengths that fall at the extremes of the range. One might have class only two times a week, not get much encouragement at home, and be somewhat overweight. The other student might have an hour-long class five times a week.

Table 2.1 is based on *reasonable estimates*. Pursuing further research will provide more objective informational guidelines, and thus the standards will be adjusted. You and your students will improve in the ability to set goals with practice setting more goals and observing the outcomes.

Table 2.1 Guidelines for Goal Setting (Amount of Change to Consider a Reasonable Goal)

Fitness component	Needs improvement	In health zone	Exceeds health zone
Aerobic endurance (1-mile run)	Decrease time 1-4 min	Decrease time 1-2 min	Decrease time 30-60 s
Flexibility	Increase reach 2-8 cm	Increase reach 2-5 cm	Increase reach 1-3 cm
Body composition	Decrease skinfold sum 1-10 mm	Decrease skinfold sum 1-5 mm	Maintain, or possibly decrease 1-2 mm
Upper-body muscular strength and endurance	Increase by 4-5 reps	Increase by 2-3 reps	Increase by 1 rep
Trunk muscular strength and endurance	Increase by 5-10 reps	Increase by 3-7 reps	Increase by 2-5 reps

Chapter 3
The Health-Related Fitness Curriculum

Although the school physical education program is not the only means to develop fitness objectives with youth, it is certainly a primary avenue. At issue is not whether we should have fitness goals in physical education but rather what those fitness goals should be and, more importantly, how we should implement them within the school curriculum. This chapter will review the National Standards for Physical Education and how to implement these recommendations into your program of health-related fitness education.

National Standards

A national consensus on the foundations of knowledge, skills, and behaviors essential to develop in physical education, adapted physical education, dance, and health education has led to national standards for these disciplines. The process has helped to update and redefine the disciplines, which subsequently have developed to include more recently identified subdisciplines. As a result of these new subdisciplines, we now have more information about skills and concepts of movement and fitness, motor development, motor learning, and exercise physiology. These are areas not traditionally found in school physical education curricula but essential for all students to enhance their potential and build the habits, attitudes, and skills that will persuade personal choice and participation in physical activity throughout life.

The national physical education standards are based on the definition of the physically educated person as defined by the NASPE *Outcomes of Quality Physical Education Programs* (NASPE 1992). According to this document,

A physically educated person:

- Has learned skills necessary to perform a variety of physical activities;
- Is physically fit;
- Does participate regularly in physical activity;
- Knows the implications of and the benefits from involvement in physical activities;
- Values physical activity and its contributions to a healthful lifestyle.

The designers intended that all five component parts of the definition not "be separated from each other" (NASPE 1992, p. 6). This definition was further defined in 20 written outcome statements with multiple benchmarks at every other grade level. The writing of *Moving into the Future: National Standards for Physical Education* (NASPE 1995) began with the intent of developing assessment guidelines for determining achievement of the outcomes. Instead, the result was the compacting of the outcome statements into seven standards to assist in designing pre-K–grade 12 assessments that would determine student achievement toward becoming a "physically educated person." Sample benchmarks, which provide ideas about what might be assessed and achieved, are included to help assess whether the standards are met at specific grade levels.

The standards should be viewed as a whole, regardless of the application or focus on either movement or fitness, the major content areas of physical education. However, to apply the standards in school instructional programs requires some deliberate analysis and isolation of concepts and skills. This analytical application is important to plan for sequential learning, which in turn leads to integrating the parts and then realization of the whole.

The *U.S. Surgeon General's Report on Physical Activity and Health* (1996) reinforces the holistic concept of "a physically educated person." This research-based publication identifies factors that determine the likelihood that physical activity will be initiated and maintained throughout life, including perceived benefit, enjoyment, feelings of competence, safety, access, time, cost, negative consequences (e.g., injury, negative peer pressure, self-identity), and use of labor-saving devices (see p. 46). The report lists "influencing and modifiable determinants" affecting physical activity behaviors among children and adolescents. Some examples of them are self-efficacy, perceptions of sports competence, expected and perceived benefits, negatively associated barriers, intention, enjoyment, favorable attitudes toward physical education, social influences of role models, availability of equipment, and time spent outdoors (p. 234). This report provides a strong message about what school and community programs must do for students to prepare them to live quality lives.

Inclusion and the Physical Education Curriculum

- No students should have to earn their ways into physical education. It is a school's responsibility to justify why a student with disabilities should be removed from regular physical education.

- Many students with disabilities have unique learning and motor needs. Some students might need modified instruction or goals and might derive different benefits from physical education. A student with mental retardation might need extra verbal cues and demonstrations to understand directions, for example. Another student might work on such individually prescribed skills as improving upper-body strength for pushing, speed, and accuracy in her wheelchair. A blind student might benefit more from the interaction and support of peers during physical education, which can motivate him to try a new skill, such as walking independently. A physical education teacher usually can meet these special needs within typical physical education situations.

- Support staff is needed for both the students with disabilities and the physical educator. Support for students might be providing monthly meetings with an adapted physical education teacher, specialized equipment, or a full-time teacher assistant.

- Removing a student from regular physical education class should be discussed only after attempts made within regular physical education have proved unsuccessful in providing necessary support to the student.

—The National Association for Sport and Physical Education (NASPE) and The American Association for Active Lifestyles and Fitness (AAALF)

Many factors in today's society lure young people from activities that are physical to pursuits that are more sedentary. Less instructional time for physical education, poorly conceived instructional programs, and less direct and inadequately trained curricular supervisors are some factors in the schools. At the same time, greater access to sedentary and technology-based entertainment, leisure activities, and work reflect influences outside the school directly competing with the factors that influence students' developing habits of participation in physical activity.

We must advocate more instruction time for physical education, but first we must improve programs.

The Physical Best educational materials have been written to help teachers deliver the essential content identified by the national standards. The materials, presented sequentially, are designed for students to master them in ways that will positively influence their choices for physical activity throughout life. The program resources are related to national standards and identify the factors that link movement, fitness, health, and the aesthetics of leisure activities and the arts.

National Physical Education Standards

The National Physical Education Standards (NASPE 1995) apply directly to fitness education programs such as Physical Best. Physical education's uniqueness lies in the skills and concepts required for successful performance in all movement forms, including fitness activities for exercise and conditioning programs. Developing movement skills and concepts has multiple purposes and benefits beyond health-related fitness in such arenas as competition, cooperation, and aesthetics. And it is the composite of all these factors that influences participation in physical activity.

The first four standards relate to fitness education in ways that are specifically identified within each instructional idea found in these materials. Some standards have a primary relationship to the unique content of physical education. Others have a secondary relationship, and they affect participation in physical activity but also have similar significance in other disciplines.

Primary Relationship.   These are the standards that directly relate to the concepts and movements of good physical education:

Standard 1.   Demonstrates competency in many movement forms and proficiency in a few movement forms.

Standard 2.   Applies movement concepts and principles to the learning and development of motor skills.

Standard 3.   Achieves and maintains a health-enhancing level of physical fitness.

Standard 4.   Exhibits a physically active lifestyle.

Secondary Relationship.   Standards 5 through 7 have an indirect relationship with physical education in that they require the mastery of the content defined by Standards 1 through 4. It is not likely that students will achieve Standards 5, 6, and 7 without mastering 1, 2, 3, and 4. Likewise, mastering 1, 2, 3, and 4 may not be possible if the learning environment, student behaviors, and affective responses to students do not foster motivation to enhance learning and instill habits. You can relate Standards 5, 6, and 7 generally to all subject areas taught in schools. Attention to them simultaneously with the more specific, content-related standards is essential to counteract factors that often negatively influence participation in physical activity.

Standard 5.   Demonstrates responsible personal and social behavior in physical activity settings.

Standard 6.   Demonstrates understanding and respect for differences among people in physical activity settings.

Standard 7.   Understands that physical activity provides opportunities for enjoyment, challenge, self-expression, and social interaction.

National Health Education Standards

The National Health Education Standards published in *Achieving Health Literacy* (Joint Committee on National Health Education Standards 1995) are linked to the physical education standards. Health education affords unique knowledge about health, preventing disease, and reducing risk factors in all situations and settings—and it influences behaviors that promote these aims. They include not only physical activity but other areas of personal, family, and community life.

Primary Relationship.   Health Standards 1, 2, 3, and 4 are most closely related to fitness education. Students will:

Standard 1. Comprehend concepts related to health promotion and disease prevention.

Standard 2. Demonstrate the ability to access valid health information and health-promoting products and services.

Standard 3. Demonstrate the ability to practice health-enhancing behaviors and reduce health risks.

Standard 4. Analyze the influence of culture, media, technology, and other factors on health.

Secondary Relationship. Standards 5, 6, and 7 could be related to any discipline including fitness education within physical education.

Standard 5. Demonstrate the ability to use interpersonal communication skills to enhance health.

Standard 6. Demonstrate the ability to use goal-setting and decision-making skills to enhance health.

Standard 7. Demonstrate the ability to advocate for personal, family, and community health.

National Standards for Dance Education

The National Standards for Dance Education (NDA 1995) are closely linked to physical education. Dance is both a movement form (as are sports, aquatics, fitness activities, and outdoor recreational activities) and a physical activity providing health and fitness benefits. Its uniqueness as a physical activity, however, is that it also is an art form, affording opportunities to create, communicate meaning, and interpret cultural issues and historical periods. Movement fundamentals found in dance are recognized as the foundations for all other movement forms. They are closely related to the development of all motor skills and movement performances.

Primary Standards. All of the dance standards relate to the understanding of movement forms in general. For purposes of these materials Standards 1 and 6 are of primary importance. Standard 6 relates to the specific fitness needs of dance performers.

Standard 1. Identifying and demonstrating movement elements and skills in performing dance.

Standard 6. Making connections between dance and healthful living.

Secondary Standards. These standards relate closely to the structure of all movement forms. They permit learning in a noncompetitive approach that focuses on structure, critical thinking, creativity, communication, and the integration of multiple disciplines. These factors help build confidence and competence in movement performances, prior to competitive involvement. The *U.S. Surgeon General's Report on Physical Activity and Health* clearly identifies these factors as critical and modifiable factors that influence participation in physical activity.

Standard 2. Understanding choreographic principles, processes, and structures.

Standard 3. Understanding dance as a way to create and communicate meaning.

Standard 4. Applying and demonstrating critical and creative thinking skills in dance.

Standard 5. Demonstrating and understanding dance in various cultures and historical periods.

Standard 7. Making connections between dance and other disciplines.

Integrating the national standards in physical education, health, and dance provides an important way to promote the effects of physical activity on health and one's personal choice to be physically active. None of these disciplines stands alone. Few student groups are solely focused on just one purpose, whether it be health, competition, or aesthetics. While some students have a greater interest in, more facile learning style for, flair for, or yearning after one of these areas, all youngsters benefit from learning and applying these standards. The recognition of these interdisciplinary links helps us maximize our energies for teaching and learning the essential content of them all.

Sequential Learning Plan

Each of the standards documents is sequential. The standards you have read here have additional, sequentially written transitional standards from one grade or school level to the next, leading to completion of the program standards. Physical education standards are designated for grades K, 2, 4, 6, 8, 10, and 12; health standards for grades 4, 8, and 11; and dance standards for grades 4, 8, and 12. Regardless of the grade designation, developing the content stepwise will enable mastery of both concepts and knowledge. Teachers should identify even smaller chunks of information and skill development. They can use these more detailed bits to plan instruction according to the developmental stage and progress of their individual students. Written instructional courses, units of study, and individual lesson plans provide the details to effectively make these developmental connections. The Physical Best materials provide you with sample ideas of useful activities that assist teachers in delivering these "smaller chunks."

General expectations for each of these levels can be found in other resources as well. For instance, the "Premises," established by the Outcomes Committee to provide direction for the writing and implementation of NASPE's *Outcomes of Quality Physical Education Programs* (Premise 11, p. 9)—and later for the writing and implementation of the physical education standards—have identified expectations level by level. Various state departments of education also provide direction and a rationale for establishing a sequence of learning, identifying in their curricular and regulatory documents the unique responsibilities particular to each grade or school level. These are general guidelines for grade-level emphases:

All grades	Physical fitness, movement skills, concepts, and affective development.
Primary grades	Movement-skill acquisition and awareness of the effect of physical activity on the body.
Intermediate grades	Movement-skill acquisition and identification and definition of specific fitness factors and their relationship to specific types of activities.

Middle school   Mastery of common physical activity skills and strategies; concepts of physical fitness training and conditioning; skills and fitness development; awareness of personal factors influencing the personal choice of physical activity.

High school   Integration of physical fitness concepts and strategies, health fitness status, and needs for physical activity performance.

Teaching any one of the many content areas in isolation from other areas gives you only short amounts of time to spend with it. So, even though teachers do not have expertise in all curricular areas, their basic knowledge of each should stimulate creative ways to make connections between the various areas. Here are a couple of ways to maximize, even making daily, the focus on fitness concepts, skills, and activities:

• Seek out teachers in other disciplines within the school, investigating essential content being taught by each, sharing essential content being taught in the physical education class, and providing creative activities that link fitness concepts to other subjects taught in the school.

• Create a fitness corner in the school library, cafeteria, or another public area. Include both factual and lifestyle information, such as a detailed breakdown of an athlete's diet and workout schedule for a full day. The display can challenge students to find out about other athletes or compare their own (or their family's) diet and activities to the athlete's. These displays should not be just athletes—include actors, entertainers, even yourself!

School is the work of children and adolescents, just as a job or career is the work of adults. Whatever their ages, people must become more aware of how they can deliberately include physical activity in their personal daily agendas—in ways that are habit-forming. That will not happen unless the plan to include it is developed and maintained at every stage of our lives, including K-to-12 school programs.

Specific Activities and Activity Modifications

Some of the activity suggestions have been adapted from *Dynamic Physical Education for Elementary School Children* and *Physical Best and Individuals with Disabilities*.

Aerobic Endurance

• Allow individuals to run or walk for time rather than distance.
• Use peer tutors or buddies to help set the pace for the activity.
• Use equipment that may help motivate individuals to continue to move.
• Engage in activities that encourage individuals to move for as long as possible.
• Let students pick out music for aerobics routines.

Upper-Body Strength and Endurance Activities

• Provide activities that encourage students to pull their own body weight.
• Develop obstacle courses that require students to pull themselves up and over obstacles.
• Use bands or terry-cloth wrist weights to increase arm strength.
• Have individuals maintain a crab or push-up position for as long as possible.

Lower-Body Strength and Endurance Activities

• Practice a variety of abdominal activities.
• Do partner sit-ups.

Flexibility

• Place objects at individuals' feet to encourage their reaching down for them.
• Use lightweight, colorful scarves that can be tossed in front of and to the side of the body; encourage the individual to reach for the scarf. Consider also using gymnastic ribbons.

Therefore, daily physical activity must be planned for all grades in school (and deliberate attention and access later given to physical activity in the workplace).

State Standards and Curriculum Regulations

Standards and curriculum regulations are written within state government, a political context. These documents may not include enough essential content or provide the conditions necessary to achieve it as identified by national standards. Why? State and local documents must address the understanding, expectations, resources, and needs of many constituent groups—not only those who are professionally trained but also lay persons called upon to support the educational system and its programs. Standards must be achievable by *all* students. Often the expectations are based on the varied experiences and visions of the lay persons or politicians who approve them.

Local school-district standards usually reflect locally acceptable expectations, cultures, and the unique resources of the community being served. When writers and teachers set up curriculums, they should use national standards to provide a content-inclusive foundation on which local school districts can interpret state standards. For classroom teaching to be effective, it must be directed by knowledgeable, up-to-date professionals who have studied the disciplines and can interpret state and local standards to deliver essential content to all students. Physical activities come in many types, but they may present similar benefits of achieving and maintaining healthful levels of fitness. Students in our classes come from varied backgrounds and with different preferences for physical activity. When these students make decisions about participating in physical activity, they are directly influenced by experiences in physical education classes. "Essential content," therefore, must include developing competence in activity skills and understanding of the concepts common to any physical activity choices students may subsequently make.

Physical and health educators are responsible, therefore, for maintaining a high enough level of expertise to be able to interpret state standards. Through them instructional programs can deliver essential content that represents the totality of the disciplines as identified by national standards. The Physical Best program, focused in fitness education, provides instructional materials to do just that.

Chapter 4
Teaching Principles for Health-Related Fitness

Physical education has many purposes, ranging from developing motor (e.g., throwing or catching) and social (e.g., cooperation) skills to learning exercise training principles. All these purposes aim to help students develop into physically active adults. Other parts of the physical education curriculum teach students cognitive information about physical fitness concepts, involve them in learning experiences to apply the fitness information, and guide them toward valuing an active, fitness-oriented lifestyle. These activities and concepts taught in class are designed to help children develop into "physically educated" people. The *National Content Standards in Physical Education* (AAHPERD 1996) state that a physically educated person "exhibits a physically active lifestyle" and "achieves and maintains a health-enhancing level of physical fitness."

Physical Best supports the program goals of the National Standards: to instill in children and youths the knowledge, skill, and attitudes that will prepare and encourage them to engage in appropriate physical activities throughout their lifetimes. Using the goals of the National Standards and the Physical Best programs as a guide, teachers can design yearly and daily plans to incorporate appropriate learning activities related to physical fitness.

Characteristics of a Quality Physical Education Program

Quality physical education programs are structured so that the duration, intensity, and frequency of activities help motivate students and meet their individual needs. When appropriate, students participate in selecting activities from all movement categories. All students have an equal opportunity to participate in a balanced physical education program. A quality physical education program will

- foster the development of positive attitudes;
- foster active participation;
- require problem-solving skills;
- recognize differences in students' interests, potential, and cultures; and
- develop personal and career-planning skills.

A good physical education curriculum also balances health-related physical fitness, motor skills, content knowledge, and personal and social development activities. To develop a quality fitness plan Virgilio (1997) makes these suggestions to physical educators:

- Plan, communicate, and cooperate with classroom teachers, administrators, and health service professionals.
- Choose noncompetitive, developmentally appropriate fitness activities, including a wide variety of exercises and movement experiences for general body development.
- Make sure that students are physically active most days of the week at least 30 minutes a day.
- Teach the benefits of an active lifestyle throughout their lives.
- Include students of all abilities in activities.
- Emphasize rewards, not awards, using positive reinforcement and incentives to motivate instead of giving awards for levels of fitness.

- Encourage self-responsibility for fitness programs by teaching the students how to monitor their progress and set goals.
- Make fitness activities fun and enjoyable, allowing students to enjoy activities with friends and the community.
- Integrate fitness education throughout the school year in the classroom and other subject areas.
- Use a variety of teaching strategies and styles by recognizing how your students learn about physical fitness.
- Model positive exercise behaviors.

Through participating in a physical education curriculum, youngsters develop the knowledge, skills, and attitudes necessary to incorporate physical activity into regular routines and leisure pursuits to live active, healthy lifestyles. The curriculum's components involve active living, movement, and personal and social responsibility. Students learn to understand the principles and concepts that support active living, develop and maintain a personal level of functional physical fitness, and develop positive attitudes toward the pursuit of lifelong health and well-being. Movement routines teach them efficient and effective movement skills, body mechanisms, and concepts in all movement categories as well as a functional level of activity-specific motor skills. Personal and social responsibility components in the curriculum develop positive behaviors and intellectual skills through participation in physical activity.

In an effective physical education program, students learn that they need not be elite athletes to establish positive physical activity attitudes, beliefs, and behaviors for lifetime health. In a good program the teachers use various teaching strategies and styles.

Developmentally Appropriate Movements

Youths need, want, and are innately programmed to move and play. Recognizing this, educators should provide an environment conducive to physical activity for *all* students, not just those who are genetically talented or who happen to mature early. Teachers are responsible for giving all students developmentally appropriate movement activities that will increase their self-confidence and promote a healthy self-esteem. These activities are all-inclusive: everybody participates and wins. Movement and play actually prepare the brain for learning. Research conclusively indicates that when children are engaged in physical activities, the cognitive domains of the brain are naturally stimulated.

Learning experiences are designed to meet the student's physical, cognitive, and emotional needs. This is what is meant by developing the "whole child." When beginning, select one student to demonstrate the main challenge of the lesson. Proceed slowly to ensure that *everyone* understands what will be involved with the activity. Give all students the chance to participate and model for one another, but allow each student to do so as an individual with personal objectives and abilities.

Teaching Strategies

Various teaching situations have some similarities and definite differences. The differences range from the size, meeting frequency, age and abilities of students, range of equipment, and duration of a class. As a physical educator you must start with well-planned objectives, matched with appropriate activities, and effectively organized to adjust to the similarities and differences among the class's members. This section briefly describes some of the effective strategies you can implement in daily plans.

Set the Environment. Equipment placed around the area sets the stage for easy retrieval. A prearranged activity area allows teachers maximum interaction with the students. Bulletin boards and signs convey that this is an environment created for students to enter and learn. When students are greeted at the door, they know the educator is ready for class and eager to work with them. These simple actions send strong messages to learners, parents, and administrators that a teacher is well prepared and organized.

Plan and Teach Routines to Use Equipment. Each student should have individual equipment to use, rather than having to wait for a turn. An efficient system for handing out and collecting equipment can save valuable time. Equipment should be placed in a safe location around the edge of the activity areas for quick distribution to students. Students hustle as they retrieve equipment in a safe manner, move to an open space, and immediately begin working on the assigned task. It is good practice to have the students place any equipment on the floor, so it is out of their hands, while you give instructions. When an activity uses circuits or stations, equipment should be located next to each station in an orderly manner allowing the students safe movement to subsequent stations.

Use Music to Enliven Activities. Music can motivate most children to move with a smile. If you add some blank intervals between selections when you dub the music onto tape, you'll have more opportunities during playback to model, supervise, and motivate students. Well-timed musical numbers are also useful to help you measure and demonstrate the concept of overload with a gradual extension of exercise time.

Use Stop and Start Cues. The use of cues to start and stop activities will facilitate activity, use class time efficiently, and promote careful listening. The cue to stop must be easily heard and well understood, especially when students are working in groups. Upon the stop cue, students are to cease activity within five seconds. Once students are all quiet and listening, deliver or model directions quickly.

Use Class Time Effectively. Clear, short directions maximize the time you have for instruction and practice. Lengthy explanations and discussions confuse students and lose their attention. Combine a visual demonstration with verbal descriptions whenever possible. Group the students quickly by assigning partners and dividing them into their smaller groups.

Focus Student Learning. Be sure to organize your class so that you give the primary focus of the lesson top priority. Explain exactly what you want the students to learn as a result of the experience or activity. The students' attention should focus on the planned outcome. Students engage in active learning when the purpose of the activity is clear, and it is effective for you to use a phrase or "mental set" to gain their focus. Visual aids encourage and reinforce learning; adding them to verbal directions allows students to utilize more than one sense. Signs with simple printed directions and pictures provide visual learners with more easily assimilated information.

Give Positive Reinforcement.   Positive feedback gives the students reinforcement. You can use it effectively even when they are progressing slowly. Positive experiences and sensing continual progress toward personal and realistic goals are important. Specific feedback directs students in helpful directions.

Integrate Activities With Other Studies.   It is important to follow a conceptual format, one that gives students experiences that will help them apply their physical education to the world outside of the classroom. Students benefit from opportunities to solve problems relating to physical activity and program development. Integrating real-world lessons and concepts, such as math or geography, also enhances the overall learning process in physical education.

Check Often for Understanding.   If you quickly invite students to pantomime a task, explain directions to a friend, respond as a group to specific questions, or point in the direction of the station rotation, you will be able to assess their understanding of the assigned task before they actually engage in the activity. Particularly if the activity is new, this could save time, which might otherwise be lost due to their confusion.

Supervise Actively.   The process of teaching and learning requires active supervision. This includes developing certain patterns: model the task, occasionally clarify or motivate, move through the activity areas, keep all students in view as much as possible, and provide positive and corrective feedback specific to the assigned task. Active supervision reinforces students' on-task behaviors, enhances the quality of practice, and communicates enthusiasm.

Use Exercise Time Instead of Repetitions.   It is always a challenge to individualize learning for all the students in a class. This task becomes particularly difficult with larger classes, broader groupings of ages and abilities, and a complex, dynamic environment. Using *time* as the basis for activities, rather than number of sets or repetitions, directly addresses concerns of individualizing instruction by encouraging students to perform as many quality movements as possible. The key to this system is to get students to hold themselves accountable for quality. Active supervision and frequent interaction with students can significantly help you hold them accountable for the given task.

Add Closure.   To close a lesson give a brief overview of what the lesson attempted to do and what students accomplished. Review objectives that might be coming up in future lessons to get the class excited about the next lesson.

To reach every student requires varying your teaching style. Before selecting a particular teaching style, you must decide what the lesson's objective is, clearly identifying what you wish the students to learn. No one teaching method or style is inherently better than any other. The one you choose will depend on the objective of the lesson.

Being innovative or using a variety of techniques and styles adds excitement to learning. Mosston and Ashworth's *Spectrum of Teaching Styles* suggests many practical and easy-to-use teaching methods, including these:

Command style is useful when teaching a new activity or lesson. The teacher uses a demonstration and explanation technique. This method is time-efficient, develops listening skills, and streamlines class management.

Practice style allows the students to take on more responsibility for learning. Although the learning objectives and class content are still decided by the teacher, the students work at their own pace to perform the task. One easy way to organize several activities at one time is to incorporate the station approach, using task cards to help with instruction. Practice-style teaching affords a teacher the freedom to give individual attention as needed.

Reciprocal style allows students to "teach" other class members the objectives and lesson content chosen by the teacher. Students work in pairs in a teaching-learning partnership. Criteria checklists provide a reference for feedback during the activity. Your role as teacher is to stay neutral and act as a facilitator.

Self-check style encourages self-responsibility and self-improvement. Decisions are shifted to the learners to promote their greater responsibility. A criteria checklist (used in the reciprocal style) works well for this teaching style, which allows individuals to set their own pace better than they can with a partner.

Inclusion style emphasizes everyone's right to participate and be successful. For this style, you establish various levels of performance for each fitness activity. The teacher's role is to encourage learners to evaluate their own performances. This teaching style gives students the right to choose to enjoy mastery of a particular level before moving on. Task cards help implement the learning activities.

Guided Discovery and Problem Solving

In guided discovery, you (as teacher) establish a predetermined answer to a problem. Then you plan a series of questions and responses to lead students (as learners) to a particular final answer. In the problem-solving style, on the other hand, the answers are unlimited. In either case, you must monitor the class for safety and organization.

Research has shown that traditional fitness-education models and strategies have been unsuccessful in developing lifetime physical activity patterns. Emphasizing how physical education is taught and using the suggested teaching styles and strategies will offer a number of more effective avenues to encourage lifelong fitness patterns among students.

Holding Students Accountable.   In an ideal world all students would be self-motivated learners, and the teacher would simply be a resource person to assist the students in pursuing their personal growth. With some students, this model holds. More often, however, students at all levels need a teacher's encouragement along the way. Your clear communication of the outcomes you expect from learners—through focus statements, prompts, and feedback—will encourage students to stay focused on learning and behavior. Your proximity to students during practice further assists youngsters with on-task behavior. This proximity is part of active supervision.

Actively Monitor Students' Progress.   As students engage in learning, move throughout the area, observing and fine-tuning their performance by giving specific task-related feedback. By scanning the area and observing students closely, you can determine the need for further group instruction to clarify a task. Or you may discover it is time to move the class on to the next planned task, having assessed that students have already reached the objective.

Question, and Summarize the Lesson.   You can intersperse questions throughout the lesson, posing them to individuals or the entire class to direct their learning. As closure for the lesson, quickly assess the students' understanding of the content through oral questioning, pantomiming performance, or a quick written response.

Don't Forget the Fun.   Young adults view social interaction and fun as important ingredients in their lives. When an activity is nonthreatening, success-oriented, and fun, students naturally become motivated. Don't be afraid to allow your students to choose accompanying music—within reason—or laugh and talk while engaged in physical activity. They will tune into class objectives while they are having fun and enjoying the lesson.

Evaluating

Evaluation is an important part of the learning experience in physical education. Choosing to be physically active for a lifetime is an ongoing process of developing motor skills, understanding principles of health-related fitness, setting personal goals, and becoming intrinsically motivated to meet self-designed goals. Therefore, the evaluation process for personal fitness must be ongoing, process oriented, and, at some point, personally significant to the individual students.

The evaluation process should be integrated throughout your planning and implementing of instructions. It

Making Objectives Inclusive

Establishing a good objective for a lesson is much more difficult when the class includes a wide range of abilities, particularly cognitive differences. Just as you must vary your teaching style, you must sometimes vary your objective style to reach all students.

When setting objectives, you'll need to adapt the broad national objectives (such as improving cardiovascular endurance) to the particular needs of your class and each student. Instead of a typical activity such as jogging, a student in a wheelchair may do laps around a hardtop track, while another student with a visual impairment may jump rope in place (Craft 1996). An over-detailed objective that requires jogging as the method of improving cardiovascular endurance would fail to include these students and fail to assist them in meeting the national standard.

One tool for making objectives inclusive is limiting group size. Controlling group size can greatly enhance the learning experience. Smaller groups allow you to tailor the objectives to the members of a particular group, and may also allow you to use unidirectional peer tutoring in appropriate circumstances. Even students as young as third grade are capable of observing and correcting one another's movement errors (Mosston and Ashworth 1994). Smaller groups rotating through different activity stations also helps maximize time on task and may help students with deficit disorders by varying environmental input.

An Individual Education Plan (IEP) offers another tool for making objectives inclusive. The IEP should note a student's significant sensory or processing deficits. You can use this information to determine appropriate objectives for that student.

Remember to avoid cultural and gender barriers to creating appropriate objectives. For example, it is inappropriate to create an objective with a specific time goal for a flexed-arm hang. This performance-based goal emphasizes muscle groups that do not develop equally across genders as adolescence approaches.

is also something to consider as you choose strategies and styles for teaching. If you have clearly identified the objectives related to fitness skills, knowledge, and behaviors in the planning process and if students have been directed in activities that match those objectives, the evaluation becomes integrated with the doing of the activity and the practice of the skills. By your active supervision, checking for understanding, and class closure, you can accomplish daily evaluations of lesson objectives.

The quality of the teaching determines the effectiveness of a fitness curriculum. In addition to pedagogical skills, teachers must value fitness and enthusiastically implement fitness lessons. You must constantly monitor teaching practices and effectiveness to keep the activities stimulating, motivating, and fun. You accomplish high quality by using developmentally appropriate activities with a lot of activity time, high levels of success, and by reinforcing and rewarding efforts.

Assessment produces information. You then use this information to further the effectiveness of your teaching. Performance categories are easy to measure and are almost always easy to define. The number of push-ups completed or laps run are easy to measure and define. Some social characteristics, such as cooperation and sportsmanship, are more difficult to define and therefore still harder to measure reliably. Assessing the simplest concepts in class, such as "We enjoyed aerobics class today," provides an evaluation tool for your teaching practices.

Effective teaching is primarily about what happens to the students. Its main ingredients are keeping students appropriately engaged in the subject matter a high percentage of the available time within a warm, nurturing climate. Learning goals are one way to assess the effectiveness of your teaching.

A *learning goal* is simply a statement of expectations for what students will learn within the school setting, given the constraints of the students' abilities and the teacher's expertise. All physical education teachers can and should have learning goals for their students. As you set and meet realistic goals, you convince yourself and your students that learning is truly part of the program. Review these guidelines as you think about writing learning goals for yourself:

- Write realistic goals.
- Write goals that you want 75 percent of your students to attain.
- Design rubrics to measure goal progress.
- Write learning goals for each unit and each grade.
- Write goals that build on your students' current levels of achievement.
- Limit the number of goals you write.

Teachers can learn a lot about themselves and their expectations for their program as they write realistic learning goals. Often curricular decisions between two important content topics hinge on the teacher's assessment of what the students should learn in order to be involved in an active, healthy lifestyle and become good citizens of the school and community. When physical educators teach from learning goals and students see their own improvement, all are likely to become more interested and motivated.

The ultimate evaluation of whether fitness education is successful comes if and when students choose to be physically active and use the skills and knowledge developed in their school years. Extending the lesson activities to encourage participation in physical activities beyond the physical education class should be integrated into the total fitness-education program.

Summary

Siedentop (1991, p. 7) defines pedagogy as "the skillful arrangement of an environment in such a way that students acquire specific intended learnings. Pedagogy links the teacher's actions with the student's outcomes." Teaching fitness to children should help them acquire the skills, knowledge, and attitudes that lead to a lifetime of physical activity. Learning should occur in all three domains of human development: psychomotor, cognitive, and affective. Fitness training is a long-term process of educating students about physical fitness and the importance of regular activity. Physical educators choose varied strategies and styles that are developmentally appropriate and effective for the particular student population to reach the goal of pursuing lifetime fitness.

Chapter 5

Managing a Health-Related Fitness Program

You must juggle many logistical aspects to teach health-related fitness effectively and efficiently. In this chapter we'll explore many of these aspects, including how to

- strike an appropriate balance between fitness activities and fitness concepts;
- collaborate with volunteers, classroom teachers, and community programs;
- obtain and store equipment;
- manage behavior through prevention and timely troubleshooting; and
- keep students safe.

You can use this concise guide to help you manage your classes more effectively.

Striking a Balance

Some teachers think fitness education presents only two scenarios:

1. They might spend too much time on health-related fitness concepts in class, and then won't have enough time to engage their students in physical activity itself.
2. They might limit the time they spend covering health-related fitness concepts and concentrate on keeping students physically active during physical education, but then they won't equip students with the necessary knowledge to be physically active and fit for life.

How can you balance the teaching of concepts and the need for actual physical activity? In this section we'll discuss how to expand your students' physical activity time while still teaching them health-related fitness concepts. Keep in mind the cycle illustrated in figure 5.1 as you study this information.

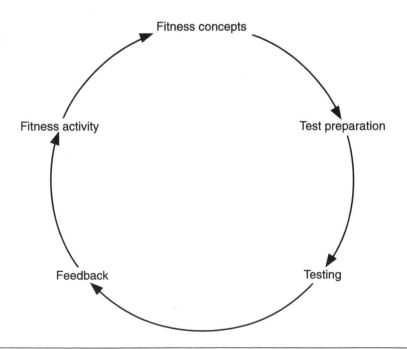

Figure 5.1   The fitness education cycle.

Kill Two Birds . . .

You'll notice that many of the activities in this book involve teaching health-related fitness concepts in a very physically active way. Not only does this "kill two birds with one stone," it also increases the likelihood that students will remember what you're teaching. Indeed, we all remember much better when we actually *do* something as part of learning it. So use the lessons in this book as a model to create your own efficient lessons. Then look beyond physical education class time to further enhance your fitness program.

Keep in mind that teaching health-related fitness does not preclude teaching other movement forms and skills. Middle school and high school students make many independent decisions about activities, especially during unscheduled times such as before and after school. Encourage students to make their choices in light of fitness concepts. For example, have students monitor their heart rates during a dance class, and discuss fitness as it relates to dance.

Creative Scheduling

You can work with administrators and other teachers to both schedule additional times for fitness activities and use existing times more fully. The following is a list of ways to increase physical activity time at school so that you can afford to spend more time on fitness concepts during class.

- *Intramurals.*   These are physical activity programs conducted between teams of students in the same school. Adapt a program to augment your fitness curriculum in specific, stated ways; work to ensure the program is fun and friendly, welcoming all who wish to participate. When creating teams, be sure to make them as even as possible. Then insist that participants focus primarily on skill, fitness, and social development, not on cutthroat competition. You can run intramural activities before or after school. Find what works for your situation and garner the support you need from people at school and home to run the kind of program that will help students see fitness as a fun, lifetime pursuit.

- *After-school programs.*   You can expand any program you normally run during the school day to fill the after-school time slot. Consider creating a new program or working to enhance an existing after-school physical activity program. If you cannot commit the time to after-school activities, train others who can, such as parents or senior volunteers. After-school programs can also include evening and weekend activities, such as family fitness nights or developmentally appropriate field days emphasizing fun physical activities instead of competition.

Note that these ideas should all serve as *extensions* of physical education, not as replacements. So make sure that your administration and colleagues understand your intent.

Fitness Homework

You can introduce a fitness concept in physical education class, assigning homework to reinforce the concept. Use the many projects in this book to involve students in worthwhile physical activity outside of school. Make sure the projects you develop involve the students in applying what they have learned in class to the real world (see figure 5.2).

Collaboration

You can and should make full use of volunteers, classroom teachers, and community programs to enhance your health-related fitness program. When using other people in your program, take the time to train them so that their approaches and attitudes match those of your program. Likewise, ensure that any community programs you tap into will respect and reinforce your philosophy. Then enjoy the enthusiasm and knowledge all these resources bring to your program.

Volunteers

Parents, older students, senior citizens, or any other interested, responsible individuals can make good volunteers. If volunteers will be working one-on-one with students, you must train them to be effective, including teaching them how to give general, specific, and corrective feedback and how to physically assist a student. Then you must give them chances to practice in simulated class situations. Guest speakers and demonstrators, such as a mother who teaches aerobics or a father who plays tennis, are also excellent resources.

Classroom Teachers

Sometimes your greatest ally in the quest to improve the fitness levels and understanding of your students is a classroom teacher. Your colleagues can set up lessons that reinforce the science and math of health-related physical fitness. Offer them specific ideas that they can tailor to their students' abilities and other studies. Some examples are calculating heart rate, learning about the cardiorespiratory system, learning about geography by actively "traveling" from one place to another, and so on. In addition, consider offering specific lesson plans for teachers to follow on days you do not teach physical education to their students.

Some specialists find it relatively easy to persuade classroom teachers and school administrators to extend meaningful physical activity into the rest of the school day. Others, however, struggle to overcome the perception that physical activity is just a way to allow students to blow off steam (or even a complete waste of time). How can you overcome such attitudes? Start slowly, asking for what you feel should be relatively easy for the classroom teacher to do. Provide support materials, such as activity and task worksheets. Your enthusiasm will be contagious if you are sensitive toward nonspecialists' fears and misperceptions regarding physical activity. To this end, provide adequate in-service training to give classroom teachers the information, support, and motivation they need to help you enhance students' fitness and knowledge about fitness. When classroom teachers see the physical and academic benefits of regular physical activity and of students' understanding how important fitness is as a lifetime pursuit, you should have the support you need.

Community Programs

Exposing students to physical activity programs in the community can be the ideal way to demonstrate that fitness is a lifetime pursuit that goes beyond the confines of school. To use these valuable resources, you can bring in visitors for demonstrations, talks, and lessons. Or you can take students on field trips to see

May 1999: FITNESS MONTH

Monday	Tuesday	Wednesday	Thursday	Friday	Saturday	Sunday
						Try a day without television. Do something outside instead. **1**
To be totally fit, nutrition is important also. Eat from all levels in the food pyramid each day. **2**	Go for a 30-minute walk with a friend. Yes, the dog can count as your friend. **3**	When you choose a snack today make it a healthy snack. **4**	Ride your bike for 30 minutes. Tell a parent where you are going. Make sure you use hand signals and follow the laws of the road. **Be safe!** **5**	The heart pumps about 7 quarts of blood per minute. Plug the sink and dump in 7×4 cups of water to see how much volume is 7 quarts. **6**	Make up an exercise routine & put it to music. Pump up your muscles, not the volume. **7**	**8**
Walk to school instead of getting a ride. **9**	Always warm up when exercising. Start slowly then stretch. Warm muscles work better. Cool down also. Do not stop suddenly. **10**	When going to the store park far away from the store. **Walk!** **11**	The best time to drink liquids is *before* you get thirsty. Sip some water before you exercise. Continue drinking water during and after exercise. **12**	Fitness is being the best **you.** Competing against others has nothing to do with fitness. Do it for yourself. **13**	Try a carryover (lifetime) sport this weekend. Go to the driving range & hit some golf balls. Go to the tennis court & hit some tennis balls. Fitness comes in all shapes & sizes just like us. **14**	**15**
Exercise helps you to fall asleep more easily at night. **16**	Organize a pickup basketball game. **17**	How many bones make up your skeleton? If you said 207 you were right. It takes a lot of muscles to move around 207 bones. **18**	Go to the nearest basketball hoop & play **Around the World, "21",** or try 25 free throws. **10**	All exercises are not created equal. Some build strength. Some build stamina. Some build flexibility. **£0**	Mow the lawn and rake the clippings for 30 minutes. Wear gloves & watch out for blisters. Jump in & over the grass piles. Bag the clippings. **£I**	**££**
Play catch with a (1) football, (2) softball, (3) Frisbee, (4) dog. Don't throw the dog, throw something to the dog. **23**	Exercise helps you do better in school. Yes, you still have to study but you are less stressed & more relaxed & ready to learn. **24**	Visit a health club. **25**	When you are physically fit you have more energy for work and play. **Exercise = Energy.** **26**	Create a fitness rap or poem. Give it to your physical education teacher. **27**	Try walking up & down the stairs for 10 minutes without stopping. **Use the handrail & keep a slow steady pace.** **28**	You need sleep to remain healthy. **Try it; you might like it.** **29**
Memorial Day Celebrate the holiday with the fitness activity of your choice. **30**	You should drink lots of water (8 glasses) especially when the weather is warm. Pop or soda does not count as water. **31**	Take care of your body, it is the only one you will get.				

May 1–7 PHYSICAL EDUCATION WEEK
GET PHYSICAL . . . . EDUCATION

Figure 5.2 A fitness month calendar.

and experience local facilities, such as a fitness center or the YMCA, and to learn about opportunities to be physically active outside of school.

Equipment

Obtaining and storing an adequate supply of equipment can be daunting tasks, but they're essential to running an effective fitness program. In this section we'll briefly describe how you can tackle this important aspect of your job.

Obtaining Enough Equipment

Effective class management and maximal time on task, both of which lead to maximal learning and fitness gains, depend largely on students having the equipment they need to be active during most of the class time. A little creativity, persistence, and planning can help you obtain enough equipment to effectively teach health-related physical fitness (Davison 1998). Here are several ways to garner additional equipment:

• *Finding free equipment*—obtain sound hand-me-downs from high schools or colleges, athletic teams, and fitness centers; obtain donated equipment from fitness equipment stores in exchange for mentioning their generosity to parents.

• *Raising funds*—organize creative fitness activities for which students obtain sponsors, family fitness nights with a small admission fee, PTA or PTSO support, and so on.

• *Making equipment*—make sit-and-reach boxes, jump ropes, markers for running courses, throwing targets, and streamers, to name a few.

• *Having students bring their own equipment*—bringing balls, jump ropes, and so on—can help augment your supply. Make sure students put their names on their equipment to prevent misunderstandings and losses. It is prudent to use this equipment only within the owner's class to better protect it.

Wherever you obtain equipment, you must ensure it is the appropriate size to foster success and that it is otherwise safe to use. If possible, accept all donations graciously so as not to discourage a donor's generosity—you never know when someone will come through with a valuable item. However, discard any items that are too worn or damaged to repair for safe use.

Collaborating with athletics programs to obtain and organize fitness equipment can help both programs. For example, strength-training equipment for the football team probably sits unused through most or all of the school day. Physical educators and coaches can get more and better equipment for both the teams and the students at large by cooperating to create a "health and fitness club" that is useful for both your health-related fitness program and the coaches' strength and conditioning programs (Human Kinetics 1998).

You can also organize lessons into learning stations to stretch an inadequate supply of equipment. That way, if you have only one sit-and-reach box, for example, you can rotate an entire class through a sit-and-reach station, keeping everyone active at other stations as they wait to use this equipment. Learning stations have other advantages, such as enhancing social interactions and allowing you to focus on one small group at a time while still engaging the rest of your students in appropriate activity.

Creating a Complete Collection

The following is a basic list of items you need to run a viable fitness program. Ensure that you have enough of each to maximize students' time on task.

- Sit-and-reach boxes
- Skinfold calipers
- Tape or CD player and music brought in by students (preview for appropriateness)
- Heart rate monitors
- Cones for marking boundaries
- Tubing or light dumbbells for strength training
- Mats
- Manipulatives for physical activities, such as balls and jump ropes
- Stopwatch

In addition, insist that students wear proper shoes and recommend that for fitness testing they wear loose-fitting clothing.

Storing Equipment

Appropriate storage can increase the longevity of equipment, facilitate class management, and save you precious time. You can make this process more efficient by

- using see-through bins, baskets, and bags whenever possible, particularly for small items;
- hanging bags from a wall or ceiling;
- organizing baskets and bins on shelves by type, unit, or other logical order;
- labeling each storage container and its place in the storage room neatly and clearly; and
- regularly inspecting equipment and repairing or replacing items as needed.

In addition, if other teachers also use the physical education equipment, develop a sign-out procedure and carefully oversee timely and accurate returns.

Managing Behavior

A natural outcome of creating and running a well-planned, well-organized, and fun fitness program is an enhanced ability to manage students' behavior. In this section we'll outline how to prevent and deal with problems that may arise—without harming kids' attitudes toward physical activity.

Preventing Problems

Thorough lesson planning can prevent many problems. In tandem with thorough planning, you can prevent most behavior problems by attending to several other important areas: establishing helpful protocols, avoiding negative practices, and motivating students. Let's look closely, now, at each of these.

Establishing Helpful Protocols. Protocols are set procedures that help you maximize students' time on task by minimizing the time wasted on noninstructional procedures, such as distributing and returning equipment and portfolios. In addition, protocols can prevent injury and misbehavior, as they establish orderly routines. The following list outlines several areas in which you should establish protocols, along with giving you helpful hints to use in forming your own specific procedures:

• *Entering and leaving the activity area.* Establish a set routine that encourages calm behavior, cooperation, and efficiency, such as entering in an orderly manner, reading posted warm-up and other instructions, and quickly following those instructions.

• *Signaling for attention and giving directions.* Choose a signal, such as blowing a whistle or beating a drum, to signal that students are to freeze, holding equipment, bodies, and mouths still so you can give them instructions. It is wise to make a rule that students gently place all equipment at their feet—to make it easier for them to leave it alone while you are speaking.

• *Distributing and collecting equipment.* Use multiple containers or have group leaders guide activities to avoid the entire class simultaneously struggling to get the equipment from one small area.

• *Assigning groups.* Use pre- and postgrouping for purposes such as fitness levels, lesson and unit objectives, and when the activity calls for homogeneous or heterogeneous groups.

• *Handling emergencies.* Train students as to what you need them to do and not do should injury, illness, or emergency occur.

Once you have designed and taught the protocols you feel you need to run the class smoothly, spend some time

Inclusion

Inclusion is a philosophy that supports placing all students with disabilities within their home school and in regular education classes. This can be a complex issue, and it has been variously interpreted by different people.

The Individuals with Disabilities Education Act (IDEA) states that individuals with disabilities should be educated in the least restrictive environment, that is, an environment that will promote the most success and the best opportunities for improving their present level of performance. In this sidebar we'll look at some ways in which you can meet the needs of individuals with disabilities during the initial inclusion phase and ongoing instructional phase.

Your attitude, approach, and organizational skills will greatly impact the chances for successful inclusion of each student with disabilities into your program. Use this checklist to help a student with disabilities make a smooth transition into your program.

• Be positive. Make the student feel a part of the class, model appropriate interactions for students without disabilities, and make efforts to accommodate the student's unique needs.

• Prepare the individual with disabilities for the integration process. Give the student time to adjust; remain fully available to resolve concerns or problems the student or her parents may have.

• Prepare students without disabilities for the process of inclusion by explaining who will be integrated and any unique needs these individuals may have. So that changes are more widely accepted, involve students in making any necessary new rules and in changing the activities for the individuals with disabilities.

• Learn as much as possible about the student with disabilities: his medications, health problems, emergency procedures, and present level of gross motor, cognitive, and affective functioning. Review the goals and objectives, unique behavior problems, and activity interests and skills listed in the Individual Education Plan (IEP) and Individualized Family Service Plan (IFSP).

• Use peers to assist you with the students who have special disabilities. Peers can help with pushing a student from station to station, making sure a student with mental retardation knows which station to go to, and giving feedback to a student with sight impairment.

• Visit other places where inclusive physical education is being implemented successfully.

having students practice them. The class time spent in practicing protocols will be made up many times over by the time saved in efficiently run lessons.

Avoiding Negative Practices. As you probably well know, your approach to health-related physical fitness will either turn your students on to physical activity or turn them off. Indeed, students who hate physical activity will not learn to enjoy it if you choose to engage in certain practices. Avoid these practices (Safrit 1995):

- Using fitness activities as punishment
- Denying (or allowing others to deny) fitness or skill education because of poor performance elsewhere in school
- Overemphasizing fitness testing
- Underemphasizing the importance of self-esteem by making negative comments about poor performance

By creating a positive learning atmosphere instead, seek to motivate students to enjoy and do their best in physical activity.

Motivating Students. Creating a fun and relevant learning atmosphere not only will reduce discipline problems, it will also increase the likelihood that students will see fitness as a worthwhile and satisfying lifetime pursuit—our central objective in bringing this program to you. What

---

Tips for Inclusion

Use this list to help make general changes in your teaching approach:

- Make simple adjustments in your teaching style choices. For example, use more demonstrations and provide more physical assistance for students with mental retardation. Avoid elimination games and modify rules so the student with disabilities can be successful. Modify equipment so students with limited strength or coordination can succeed. Use small groups and station activities with a range of challenges.
- Provide clear, concise, and brief verbal cues and demonstrations.
- Provide extra opportunities for practice.
- Observe individual behavior and provide adequate feedback, pairing positive feedback with corrective feedback.
- Maximize on-task behavior and minimize off-task behavior. For groups that include individuals with a variety of ability levels, design activities that allow them to work at their own levels.

The following are more specific guidelines for teaching individuals with disabilities:

- Use success-oriented activities.
- Incorporate an appropriate awards program.
- Post only the names of youngsters who meet their goals, rather than their actual scores.
- Increase intensity more gradually than usual.
- Modify distance goals and areas of play for individuals with limited movement abilities.
- Lower or enlarge the size of goals.
- Reduce the number of points needed to win a game.
- Use equipment that varies in shapes, sizes, and textures to stimulate interest.
- Preselect teams.
- Give individuals adequate time to process information.
- Limit distractions whenever possible.

---

motivates children? Play and fun, social interaction, feelings of physical competence, chances for self-expression, and choice. So plan these into your health-related fitness program.

Here are some specific motivational strategies you might consider (Safrit 1995):

- *Give choices.* Allow students to choose fitness activities from a menu of choices. A student might choose from aerobic dance, or basketball, or power walking, as long as the activity provides sufficient health benefits.
- *Teach basic skills.* Give students the tools they need to succeed.

Remember, fitness is a process. It's more important to continue to be active than to score high on a fitness test and then become inactive.

- *Choose success-oriented activities.*　Pay close attention to developmental appropriateness to ensure all students can succeed.

- *Have fun, fun, fun.*　Children naturally love to move, so take advantage of it. Virgilio (1997) insists, "Children should laugh, sing, play, and interact while engaged in physical activity." To add spark to your lessons, play music and choose activities that use a child's imagination.

- *Add creative equipment.*　Rotate the equipment you use to teach various concepts to renew interest in physical activity.

- *Create a colorful environment.*　Decorate the gym attractively according to your current theme.

- *Provide incentives.*　Extrinsic motivators that reward effort rather than prowess have their place in fitness education (see chapter 2).

- *Be a role model for your students, fellow teachers, and principal.*　Dress professionally in sharp-looking warm-ups or other appropriate clothes. Let students see you enjoying physical activity and eating appropriate nutrients.

- *Accentuate the positive.*　Use gestures and words of encouragement to reinforce positive behavior and increase the likelihood of progress.

- *Keep students moving and otherwise engaged.*　Minimize lecturing.

- *Encourage self-direction.*　Show students how to apply the knowledge they're learning in the real world. Teach students to manage their own fitness education portfolios, giving them the necessary tools to direct their own fitness training after they leave your program.

Fitness Is for Everyone

Health-related fitness is equally important for boys and girls. Don't lower expectations for girls! It is critical to developing a gender-equitable learning environment that you understand, monitor, and develop student-to-student interactions. These dynamics establish a student "pecking order." Without intervention, some of these interactions could be damaging to girls and boys alike. To encourage gender-equitable interactions, encourage appropriate verbal and physical interactions between students, praise positive interactions, turn both positive and negative interactions into "teachable moments," and set the stage for cooperative activities between boys and girls. When you present examples, make them of both men and women. For example, Michael Jordan has to be in great shape to be successful—and so does Mia Hamm!

You should also consider the factors that contribute to making a message and its dissemination special for a given population. Such factors might include demographic parameters, individual families' values and beliefs, the students' perceptions of engaging in a specific health activity, the channels available for communication, and the influence of community leaders and groups. In addition, be aware that clothing may present problems. Some religious tenets, for example, preclude wearing the very type of apparel that many people consider appropriate for participating in physical activity.

Most of these motivators are intrinsic. In other words, they make physical activity a reward in and of itself, thereby increasing the likelihood that students will pursue physical activity on their own. Not surprisingly, motivated students are more cooperative, making your job that much easier.

Finally, cooperative learning approaches enhance motivation by providing the social interaction students enjoy and thrive on. Moreover, students learn from each other in cooperative groups, empowering them to apply their knowledge in other situations as they practice helping each other succeed. So plan cooperative learning experiences as often as possible.

Dealing With Problems

Prevention is your watchword: You've established protocols. You've planned in appropriate motivators. You're still, however, dealing with a few problems. Don't despair—we all face similar situations. Here are some trouble-shooting hints:

- Don't allow problems to fester; deal with them quickly and decisively to prevent them from spreading.
- Modify protocols that don't seem to be working.
- Add appropriate protocols as you note the need arising.
- Engage the help of parents, classroom teachers, a special education teacher, or administrative staff when a student persistently disrupts class. Ask for insights and hints that will help this particular student experience success.
- Work out a specific plan with the student and other advisors to overcome the disruptive behavior.
- Include special incentives tailored to the particular student's interests. For example, allow the student to choose a favorite activity when he or she has cooperated to a set degree or amount.

Safety

Thorough planning, effective class management, developmentally appropriate equipment and activities, and equipment and facilities in good condition are the keys to safe physical education. Here are reminders specific to fitness education that Safrit (1995) cites:

- Have students warm up the large muscles of the body before they engage in vigorous and extensive exercise.
- Help students learn to identify the difference between fatigue and pain that may lead to injury.
- Always ensure that environmental conditions are safe for the fitness lesson.
- Educate yourself and your students as to harmful exercises. Stay up to date on safety issues.
- Make sure students are wearing appropriate clothes and shoes and that they are not wearing jewelry, such as long necklaces or earrings, that could become tangled by equipment or ensnare classmates.

Stay alert to potential dangers to *prevent* problems.

Summary

With foresight, persistence, and timely troubleshooting, you can run classes that are effective, enjoyable, and safe. Use the suggestions in this chapter to help you maximize time on task and minimize disruptions. Teach in safe and developmentally appropriate ways. Above all, keep fun as the focus of your health-related fitness program to ensure that students will want to make fitness a lifetime focus.

Chapter 6
Assessing Health-Related Fitness

You are responsible for assessing what your students have learned in physical education, based on the goals and objectives you have set. You cannot, however, achieve truly authentic assessment by basing it solely on any one indicator. Use a variety of assessment tools, including fitness tests, to create a true picture of each individual's achievements. Moreover, you must assess in all domains—physical, cognitive, and affective—by monitoring actual student performance in authentic, real-world settings. Ultimately, you must look more at the process than at the product, gathering evidence of progress over time. In other words, teach the processes you're assessing, including proper techniques and fitness knowledge. Emphasize the *how* and *why* of education, rather than stressing current physical ability, if you want to empower students to assume personal responsibility for fitness.

Yet the realities of assessment—a teacher's time commitment, organizational challenges, and limited class time, to name a few—may tempt you to avoid developing and implementing a formal approach. In this chapter we'll explore the importance of assessment, define and discuss authentic assessment, show you how to apply authentic assessment tools to fitness education (including management tips), and, finally, discuss the issues of grading.

Importance of Assessment

The most important benefits of assessment are enhancing student motivation and learning. When you emphasize self-assessment, self-responsibility, and goal setting, you motivate students to improve their performances. When you teach students the "hows" and "whys" of health-related physical fitness, you give them the knowledge they need to become responsible for their own fitness. Most importantly, however, you teach students *how* to learn—the processes of self-analysis and self-direction—something they can take with them when they leave your program. So a carefully constructed assessment approach empowers students to reach our ultimate goal—that of self-directed, active lifestyles.

Beyond this, assessment serves several other purposes. It

1. forces us to look carefully at each individual, if only for a few moments;
2. gives us an overall assessment of the program when we see the gains juniors and seniors have made since sixth grade;
3. increases our credibility as professionals when we provide recorded evidence of individual and program progress; and, finally,
4. becomes a self-imposed accountability measure, forcing us to look at the results of our teaching.

Rink and Hensley assert in summary, "Assessment is the cornerstone of education reform, enabling educators to create high-level goals, set standards, develop instructional pathways, motivate students, provide diagnostic feedback, monitor progress, communicate progress to others, and make appropriate decisions about students and programs" (1996, p. 39).

Authentic Assessment

As you probably well know, fitness testing has been widely abused by some educators in the past. As a result, many individuals insist that fitness testing has no place in the authentic assessment movement. We couldn't disagree more! In this section we'll show you how to make fitness testing a valuable part of authentic assessment.

First, however, what is authentic assessment? Assessment may be called authentic "if the student demonstrates the desired behavior in real-life situations rather than in artificial or contrived settings" (Melograno 1998, p. 10). Applied specifically in physical education, developmentally appropriate authentic assessment means that teacher decisions are based on ongoing individual assessments of students and not on a single test score. Thus, for fitness testing to be a viable component of authentic assessment, it must

1. demonstrate the desired behavior,
2. link directly to the curriculum,
3. occur on an ongoing basis, and
4. make students both capable of and likely to apply the tests and the physical gains outside the classroom.

Gains evidenced by authentic assessment should be made in the physical, affective, and cognitive domains, meaning an individual develops health-related fitness, a positive attitude, and fitness knowledge.

Putting Fitness Testing in Context

Some may argue that fitness testing is "artificial or contrived," but there is a significant correlation between performance on health-related fitness tests and actual health-related fitness (CDC 1999). Furthermore, health-related fitness testing that is part of a sound, ongoing educational program gives students the basic knowledge they need to be fit for life. Moreover, fitness testing provides a kind of "snapshot" of each individual's current fitness level, and an opportunity to plan for future improvement (in the same manner as does a math or reading test).

Measuring Progress Over Time

Of course, a single test score cannot tell you anything about an individual's progress. This is why you must plan for ongoing assessment for it to be truly authentic. But given the workload associated with testing hundreds of students, how can you accomplish this overwhelming task? One answer is to train students to assess themselves informally and to train volunteers to help you assess students who are not yet prepared for self-assessment.

These are some major benefits of training students for self-assessment:

- Teaches students specific tests they can apply throughout their lives
- Gives students guided practice in applying their knowledge of fitness testing
- Stimulates a self-directed approach to fitness
- Shows students exactly what you expect them to learn—and then teaches and assesses it, thereby linking fitness testing directly to the curriculum in students' minds
- Makes assessment time double as learning time
- Gives students ongoing feedback in the form of test results and teacher guidance

- Provides built-in respect for individual abilities and progress
- Adds ongoing input for realistic goal setting

If you have too little class time for assessments, you can send self-assessment task sheets as homework for students to complete outside of physical education class time. You know you're on to a valuable teaching practice when it saves your time and energy while helping students achieve your ultimate goals!

Peer assessment leads to the same benefits as self-assessment. In addition, peer assessment enhances social development.

Periodically, however, you should conduct formal fitness tests, rotating the classes you're focusing on and thus spreading out the paperwork. Within each class, use the learning station approach so that you can oversee a testing station, ensuring correct technique and accurate data. While assessing students, be sure to reinforce the reasons for fitness testing and fitness itself, thereby connecting this activity to real life. Figure 6.1 offers a handy checklist to ensure you're ready to formally assess students.

Preparing for Fitness Testing

- ☐ 1. Sequence the tests.
- ☐ 2. Schedule and organize testing.
- ☐ 3. Consider safety factors.
- ☐ 4. Obtain necessary equipment.
- ☐ 5. Find or design efficient scoring sheets.
- ☐ 6. Locate and train assistants.
- ☐ 7. Send a letter home to parents, letting them know the date of the tests and asking that they ensure students have necessary clothing on the testing date.

Figure 6.1 Planning for fitness testing will make your job easier (adapted from Safrit 1995, p. 78).

Applying Authentic Assessment Tools to Fitness Education

Your assessment of an individual must be based on a variety of assessment tools—not just formal and informal fitness testing—to teach and assess student progress in fitness education. This creates a balanced approach to assessment, allowing students to show you the "big picture" of their learning. Table 6.1 lists several authentic assessment tools that are appropriate, along with examples of their application in fitness education. Note, too, that these tools give students the opportunity to display different types of intelligence; a child who is weak in one form of intelligence can shine in another while still developing the weak area. Strive to use a variety of assessment tools in your program.

Let's now examine more specifically how these tools can help you assess students in the physical, cognitive, and affective domains, discussing appropriate methods and effective uses of results.

Table 6.1   Appropriate Authentic Assessment Tools

Tool	Description	Example
Self-assessment	Student assesses herself based on goals or teacher-set criteria.	Student uses a sit-and-reach box to monitor flexibility between doing more formal tests.
Peer assessment	Peers observe each other's performances & offer feedback based on teacher-set criteria.	Students observe each other stretching, completing a criteria task sheet to help each other learn to stretch safely and effectively.
Journal	Student assesses himself by recording his activities or feelings in writing.	Student records each bout of physical activity he engages in outside of physical education class and notes how he feels afterward.
Reflection	Student thinks about the learning process to improve her performance & attitude.	Student lists three specific ways she can improve her one-mile run time.
Observation	Teacher observes and records physical and affective information.	Teacher monitors student testing at a learning station, rating her observations on a criteria task sheet.
Individual project	Student investigates an area of interest under teacher's guidance, setting goals, planning how to achieve those goals, & striving for those goals.	Student explores how to apply health-related fitness concepts to his favorite sport & tests his theories as to what will help improve his sport performance.
Group project	A group of students learns in a situation in which interdependence, cooperation, & accountability are required.	A group works together to design a game that builds cardio-respiratory endurance. They then teach it to another group.
Role-playing	Students assume roles & explore social & psychological issues in simulated affective activities.	Partners take turns counseling a "friend" who is reluctant to participate in physical activity.
Event task	Students problem-solve, using a type of role-playing that simulates real-world experiences & offers open-ended tasks.	The teacher challenges groups of students to design & demonstrate several ways they can use to help include a student with a disability in physical activity.

(continued)

Table 6.1   (continued)

Tool	Description	Example
Fitness testing	Give standardized tests (such as *FITNESSGRAM*) of each area of health-related fitness to help teachers & students plan how to maintain or improve each one.	Student practices muscular strength & endurance tests, takes the tests, & records the results. She then plans how she will improve over time.
Portfolio	Student collects samples of her work to show her effort, progress, & achievement over time.	Student puts her plans for improving muscular strength & endurance in writing, along with her test scores, adding this information to her portfolio.

Melograno, 1998.

Physical Domain

During periods of fitness testing and education you will assess students in the physical domain, of course, but you should also monitor their applications of the health-related fitness components when they are in skill and sport settings. In this section we'll discuss various authentic assessment tools that can help you assess student progress in the physical domain.

Useful Assessment Tools.   Fitness tests (e.g., *FITNESSGRAM*) are the most obvious and structured way to assess fitness in the physical domain. Another forum for observing students' fitness is their performing both general and sport-specific skills, allowing you to note those that are weak in one or more health-related fitness components. For example, after such observations you can work more closely with a student who lacks the flexibility or strength to master gymnastics stunts or one who doesn't have the stamina to keep running in basketball or soccer. As you look for each health-related fitness component in a real-world context, you can better tailor your program to meet individual needs. Other means of assessing students in the physical domain include

Remember, fitness is individual. Encourage children who show low levels of fitness by explaining to them that any improvement will be significant. Challenge students with high levels of fitness to do even better. Support students with significant disabilities in the activities they can engage in. In short, challenge students at their appropriate levels.

- self-assessment,
- peer assessment,
- individual projects, and
- event tasks.

In these examples you can see how fitness testing serves to confirm a teacher's concerns and helps her monitor individual progress. Thus, fitness testing can serve your program, rather than your program serving fitness testing.

Finally, always attend carefully to safety when you and your students engage in fitness testing. Figure 6.2 offers a safety checklist.

Using Results Appropriately.   We cannot emphasize too much that fitness testing must be part of your quest to individualize and otherwise im-

Safety Checklist for Fitness Testing

❑ 1. Give students plenty of chances to practice before the test.

❑ 2. Check for proper form, correcting when necessary.

❑ 3. Ensure that the test area has enough space, its surface is suitable, and is free of hazards (such as glass).

❑ 4. Provide mats for curl-ups and flexibility testing.

❑ 5. Check equipment to ensure its proper functioning.

❑ 6. Remind students of emergency procedures.

❑ 7. If you're testing outdoors, monitor environmental conditions for cardiovascular testing.

❑ 8. Have students warm up with a general cardiorespiratory activity and stretching.

Figure 6.2 Always test under safe conditions (adapted from Safrit 1995, p. 80).

prove instruction, not a contest to see who is the fittest among students. Thus, strive to use fitness testing results in the following ways (Safrit 1995):

• Be sensitive to students' feelings and keep results and records confidential, even if it means locking up files. Insist that students not share results among themselves. Finally, reward persistence, improvement, and effort—instead of elite performance.

• Relate fitness testing results to fitness education. Talk specifically about how students can improve or maintain their results. Help them plan realistic goals and steps toward those goals.

• Inform and involve parents—both before and after testing. Send information about what tests you're giving and why, emphasizing your philosophy regarding fitness testing. Explain fitness basics and the meanings of results at a parent-teacher conference, if at all possible, or at least in writing.

Cognitive Domain

The cognitive domain automatically comes into play as you empower students to take increasing responsibility for their fitness testing, goal setting, and individual fitness planning. In other words, as you teach students how to apply the fitness test results, including goal setting and planning how to improve their performances, you are asking them to think. In this section, we'll explore ways to assess individuals' progress in understanding the learning processes they are going through.

Useful Assessment Tools. When choosing cognitive assessment tools, you must select instruments that reflect what you have taught students regarding fitness knowledge and that are manageable to administer. One quick way to assess understanding is to simply observe how students perform the fitness tests and discuss this performance with them. Do they use correct technique consistently? Do quick reminders help them perform correctly or do you need to spend more time with them? When you debrief the class at the end of a testing session, do you find that the students have a good sense of why they are taking the tests and how they might improve performance? Make a statement or series of statements regarding health-related fitness and have students signal thumbs-up for true and thumbs-down for false. These methods, which don't take much administrative time or energy, can give you valuable (albeit informal) information to help guide your planning for future lessons.

Written tests are a tried-and-true way to test the cognitive domain. Include one at a station on a circuit or work with an appropriate classroom teacher, such as a health or biology teacher, to administer a short test. In any case, keep such tests short and to the point—no more than three to five multiple choice questions to give you the feedback you need without taking too much instructional or teacher time. Figure 6.3 presents a sample written test appropriate for fitness education assessment in the cognitive domain. You can also administer a longer test to assess the breadth of your students' fitness knowledge. FitSmart, which is available from the American Fitness Alliance, is designed as a national test for high school students.

Ask students to analyze their own performances; you can add a "Thinking About Learning" box at the bottom of task sheets to encourage thoughtful reflection (Melograno 1998). Make sure, however, that they feel it's safe to tell the truth about their performance assessments: emphasize the importance of process (self-analysis) rather than product (actual performance). Of course, this activity also touches on the affective domain.

Other assessment tools you can structure to reveal knowledge of fitness concepts include the following:

- Reflection in journals
- Individual projects
- Role-playing, including event tasks

Most importantly, you can use all these tools to help students learn *how to learn* as they apply the facts you've taught them in different ways.

Using Results Appropriately.   Like any authentic assessment tool, oral checks for understanding or written tests to assess cognitive development should only be a part of your whole assessment approach. Use the information you gather to help you tailor your teaching plans to both the class's abilities in general and to specific individual needs. If you wish to use written tests as part of your grading system, ensure they are just that—*part* of a system that takes many types of assessment into account (see also "Grading" later in this chapter). Finally, as you work to develop the cognitive aspects of fitness education, emphasize that students need to learn this information because health-related fitness is temporary; therefore, each one of us must become equipped to plan how to maintain or improve our own fitness level on a continuing basis.

Affective Domain

Perhaps you view the affective domain as being secondary to what your program is doing in the physical and cognitive domains—something, that is, to attend to and monitor if there's time. Don't fall into this trap! The affective domain is actually the heart of a successful program, a program that inspires enthusiasm for physical activity and a desire for fitness in each student, no matter his or her abilities or interests. Think about it this way: no matter how well-versed

Name _____   Date _____

Class _____

Aerobic Fitness Quiz

1. Michael is 17 years old. His resting heart rate is 70. He wants to improve his aerobic fitness. He carefully checks his heart rate during an exercise session. Circle the correct description for each of these heart rates:

85	Overexertion	Target Exercise Zone	Underexertion
105	Overexertion	Target Exercise Zone	Underexertion
125	Overexertion	Target Exercise Zone	Underexertion
145	Overexertion	Target Exercise Zone	Underexertion
165	Overexertion	Target Exercise Zone	Underexertion
185	Overexertion	Target Exercise Zone	Underexertion
205	Overexertion	Target Exercise Zone	Underexertion
225	Overexertion	Target Exercise Zone	Underexertion

2. Which of the following activities will help improve aerobic fitness?

   a. Walking quickly around the track or gymnasium for 10 minutes every day at lunchtime

   b. Powerlifting

   c. Mowing the lawn (about 30 minutes)

   d. Watching TV

   e. a and c only

3. How often must you exercise to improve aerobic fitness?

   a. Every day

   b. At least five days every week

   c. At least four days every week

   d. At least three days every week

   e. Once or twice a week

4. How long must you exercise during each exercise session to improve aerobic fitness?

   a. At least 60 minutes

   b. At least 40 minutes

   c. At least 20 minutes

   d. At least 10 minutes, but for a total of at least 40 minutes for the day

   e. At least 10 minutes, but for a total of at least 20 minutes for the day

Figure 6.3   Sample quiz.

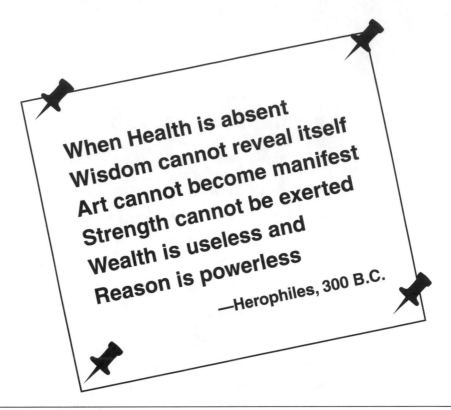

When Health is absent
Wisdom cannot reveal itself
Art cannot become manifest
Strength cannot be exerted
Wealth is useless and
Reason is powerless

—Herophiles, 300 B.C.

Figure 6.4   Bulletin board.

students are in health-related fitness concepts, no matter how many hours per week they engage in appropriate physical activity now, if they hate what they're doing, they'll surely stop it as soon as they are out of your program. So carefully assess affective development on an ongoing basis to alert you to potential problems.

Useful Assessment Tools.   You can slant various assessment tools toward assessing the affective domain. For example, ask students to reflect in their journals on what they are feeling about your program or a particular activity. Take a written or oral survey, such as the one shown in figure 6.5. Present role-playing challenges to partners and have one partner pretend to love fitness activities and the other, to hate it. You'll be amazed as you eavesdrop by how articulate students are about their positive and negative feelings. And simply being allowed to air negative feelings in a safe context can do much to dissipate them. You have no time? Use these suggestions as two-minute closure activities. Assign written assessments as homework, including regular journal entries.

Using Information Appropriately.   Obviously, you should not condemn a student for a poor attitude toward health-related physical fitness. Rather, you should seek to help that student overcome negative feelings through providing a fun program, helping the student set realistic goals, and empathizing with the student's hidden fears. This process may include helping parents overcome their negative feelings toward physical activity as well. If you notice widespread negativity, brainstorm with students and colleagues about how to make your program more fun. Keep in mind, however, that sometimes even the best programs take time to overcome bad feelings created by negative past experi-

Figure 6.5 Examples for different reflection strategies (adapted from Graham 1992).

ences. Regularly evaluate your teaching and program, then move ahead confidently and enthusiastically. Your persistence will pay off.

Portfolios—Putting It All Together

We believe portfolios can be a vital part of authentic assessment because, when well conceived and organized, they provide a handy reference for overall assessment, grading, and parent-teacher and parent-student conferences. Moreover, portfolios can travel with students from grade to grade and school to school, so that both the students and future physical educators can monitor long-term

Physical Best Activity Guide

62   Physical Best Activity Guide

progress and persistent problems. In this section, we'll focus on how you can streamline the administrative tasks associated with portfolios.

As you probably well know, the gap can be quite wide between theory and practice with authentic assessment in general and portfolio keeping in particular. Use these tips to help turn portfolios into the teaching, learning, and assessing tools they are meant to be—without your having to spend 16 hours a day at school:

• Obtain or have students or volunteers make sturdy portfolios. For each use a traditional three-hole folder, a folded piece of 12- by 18-inch construction paper with pockets added, a flat box, a hanging file, or other appropriate container.

• Store portfolios by class in milk crates, portable hanging file boxes, or larger bins.

• Train students to file their papers properly for themselves.

• Establish protocols for passing out and collecting portfolios.

• Periodically, select (or have students select) representative pieces from their assessment activities to retain in their portfolios. This leaves fewer bits and pieces for you to sort through. Designate how many pieces to select, taking the time to discuss what creates a good cross-section of items. Send the rest home after stamping them with a message such as "COMPLETED ON TIME" to indicate you do care but that you're not using it as part of your assessment of a student. This will eliminate paperwork in a professional manner. *Note*: If you designate pieces to select after the work is completed, students will be motivated to try their best on each assignment.

• Staple, tape, or glue certain ongoing assessments, such as a fitness testing record sheet, into the front or back cover of each portfolio.

• Decide whether you wish to staple in several sheets of paper to form journals inside each portfolio, use a separate notebook for journals, or add individual sheets to portfolios with journal-type entries as they are written.

Ensuring Gender Equity

Evaluations free of gender bias place equivalent expectations on females and males. In addition, evaluators can spend equal time interacting with girls and boys in praising, disciplining, instructing, and providing other types of feedback. Educators must take care that evaluative instruments are free of gender bias and that student performance is not evaluated on the basis of male experience alone.

Ask other teachers in your building and district for additional ideas regarding the logistics of sane portfolio management.

Grading

Assessing and grading are not one and the same. Indeed, they have very different purposes. Assessment tells you and your students how they are improving or what they need to work on. Grading attempts to communicate in a single letter or number, addressed primarily to parents, all that the individual student has done in your physical education program (Graham 1992). Alongside of assessment, grading can help you recognize the strengths and weaknesses of your physical education program.

In order to grade students fairly, you must develop criteria for testing and grading, including the weight you will assign each component of the grade. Then you must communicate these parameters to students and parents—*before* collecting data. Safrit (1995) makes these suggestions:

- Don't use improvement in fitness-test scores as the basis for grading unless you have provided sufficient class time for improving fitness.
- Use evidence of cognitive development as long as you have taught the concepts you're measuring.

Finally, you must collect explicit documentation to maintain accountability. A portfolio system can do much of the record keeping for you.

But a grade in physical education doesn't tell students and parents much about how an individual is doing. For example, a student who has very poor flexibility may receive a "Satisfactory" simply for behaving in physical education class and trying hard (Graham 1992). You can overcome this problem by providing separate grades for affective, physical, and cognitive performance. Develop and use your own form to send home with the rest of the report card. On this form, note areas of improvement and offer tips as appropriate about how the student can overcome problem areas. You can also use such a form at the end of each unit, whether it's grading time or not. Even if you must enter a total grade on the regular report card, by offering students and parents specific information, you will help students learn through grading, thereby making it a more worthwhile use of your time.

Indeed, objective and thorough grading should do the following:

- Help the student understand where he can improve
- Help the teacher recognize if program objectives are being met
- Show the teacher where changes in the program should occur
- Promote the physical education program to the school and community
- Justify the ongoing need for physical education in the curriculum

Summary

Assessment is an indispensable component of all effective teaching; fitness education is no exception. You can and should use a variety of assessment strategies across the fitness education curriculum to gather data on each student's achievement. Portfolios can provide the foundation of an authentic assessment approach. You can have students complete several different types of assessment tools. Managing assessment takes thought and planning but is well worth the effort.

Finally, when you give a physical education grade, you should offer specific data, well documented across the physical, affective, and cognitive domains. In this way, you will demonstrate that you do, in fact, provide a balanced, worthwhile curriculum.

Chapter 7 —

Nutrition and Health-Related Fitness

The science of nutrition defines and explains the human body's dietary need for specific chemical substances to maintain life. We all have the same general nutritional needs, but the amounts of specific nutrients that we each require vary according to age, gender, heredity, and lifestyle. Each of us has several diet options that can afford pleasurable eating while meeting individual nutritional requirements. Thus the amount of energy and the quantity of nutrients we require are best tailored individually. The challenge we each face is to obtain all the essential nutrients from our particular diets.

What Is Diet?

Diet is the total intake of food (and supplements, if taken) consumed in a five-to-seven day period. No single food or single meal defines the diet. Over a 70-year life span, a person will eat some seventy thousand meals—about a thousand each year—plus snacks. Is it any wonder that eating is automatic?

Although all foods have nutritional value—there are no "junk" foods with absolutely *no* nutritional value—clearly some foods are more valuable than others. In assuring a person good nutrition the fundamental goals are to

- provide a variety of different foods,
- supply all the nutrients in adequate amounts, and
- supply sufficient energy (calories) to maintain an ideal body mass.

There are infinite ways, which are often decided by taste, culture, and economics, for an individual to meet these dietary needs. Nevertheless, experts have developed broad, useful guidelines to encourage individuals to obtain the essential amounts of the nutrients they need to promote growth and development and to maintain an ideal body mass. These are some well-known developers of such guidelines:

- The Committee on Dietary Allowances, which establishes guidelines called the Recommended Dietary Allowances (RDA). The RDA cite the amount of each nutrient required on an average day to meet the needs of most healthy people under usual environmental conditions in the United States.

- The Food and Drug Administration, which developed a standard format for food labeling.

- The U.S. Department of Agriculture (USDA), which designed the Food Guide Pyramid to graphically show the most necessary nutrients within each food group, the number of recom-

Food Labels at a Glance

Figure 7.1   Illustration of a typical food label.

mended servings, the size of such servings, and foods within each group categorized by nutrient and density.

Behavioral Foundations of Diet

For countless generations food choices were largely determined by what people could grow (farm) or catch. During these historic times, knowing and choosing what to eat was fairly easy—people simply ate what was available. Having a much greater variety of choices today, we often find it more difficult to decide what food to eat. We must *learn* how to make appropriate choices.

All people require the same nutrients, but in amounts that vary from individual to individual and from stage to stage in a person's life. Neonatal and infant nutrition set the stage for the later interaction of home and school in influencing a child's nutritional habits. After undergoing explosive growth during the first year of life, a child continues to develop and change, but somewhat less quickly. The cumulative

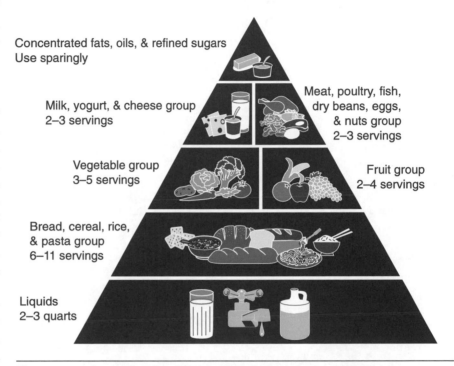

Figure 7.2   A modified Food Guide Pyramid focusing on daily intake.

effects over the next decade are remarkable. A child enters the school system at a critical stage of growth and development, which will continue through the elementary, middle, and high school years. To have a healthy diet, a child must eat food that provides all of the nutrients—(particularly iron, trace elements, calcium, protein, and vitamins) in adequate quantities over a five- to seven-day period—all the time.

The school years offer the best chance for parents and teachers to influence not only current but also future food choices, and thus to help develop good eating behaviors. Parents are the gatekeepers; they control and influence the availability and choices of food in their children's environment. Teachers must actively help educate parents about nutrition. It is critical that parents and teachers help establish appropriate eating habits and make students aware of the relationship between nutrition and health, both now and for the future. The concept of balance and moderation to obtain and maintain an ideal body weight is crucial in preventing such eating disorders as anorexia.

A person's total nutrient needs are greater during adolescence than at any other time of life except pregnancy and lactation. According to the USDA guidelines, during adolescence girls need 2,200 calories a day, whereas boys require 3,000 calories a day (Saltman, Gurin, and Mothner 1993). Nutrient needs rise throughout adolescence and then level off (or even diminish slightly) as an adolescent becomes an adult.

Adolescents make many more choices for themselves than do young children, both about their activity level and what they eat. Social or peer pressures may push them to make both good and bad choices. Children and adolescents acquire information—and misinformation—on nutrition from personal, immediate experiences. They are concerned with how diet can improve their lives and looks *now*, so they may engage in crash dieting or the latest fad in weight gain or loss. It is common also to see increased calorie consumption, especially of fats and carbohydrates, among adolescents.

Poor childhood habits in both physical activity and nutrition often lead to health problems in adulthood. For example, obese children seldom develop heart disease, cancer, or gall bladder diseases as children. However, childhood obesity may set the stage for adult obesity, when the threat of these and other diseases associated with obesity does increase.

The interactions of physical activity and nutrition are important in every person's life. We need physical activity as much as we need all 45 nutrients in our diets.

Six Fundamental Needs

There are six important nutritional concepts that you as a teacher should emphasize to students at all levels. This chapter focuses on them, relating the concepts to youths and integrating their present diet with their future development by promoting the development of good health habits now. Your task is to help students integrate the science of nutrition with their own social, economic, and cultural backgrounds so that they can develop and enjoy lifelong, healthy habits of nutrition and physical activity.

By applying knowledge from nutrition, medicine, and physiology and

---

Counting Calories

A calorie is the amount of energy it takes to raise the temperature of one gram of water one degree Celsius. The body's needs are much greater than water's, of course, so we measure energy in kilocalories (1,000 calories, or one kcal). Popular sources often shorten the term *kilocalories* to simply *calories*, which can be confusing. We will refer to calorie counts in this book, rather than using the less-familiar term kilocalorie. Different types of food have different energy values for equal weights (see table). *Nutrient density* refers to the amount of a given nutrient per calorie. A variety of foods with high nutrient densities should predominate in a diet. Basing a diet on foods with low nutrient densities, for example, risks either overeating to obtain adequate amounts of necessary nutrients or doing without those necessary nutrients.

Food	Amount	Calories
American cheese	50 gm (about two slices)	185
Fast-food fried chicken drumstick	54 gm (one)	135
Hard-boiled egg	50 gm (one large)	80
Breaded fish sticks	55 gm (two)	100
Pork (breakfast) sausage links	50 gm (three)	185
Flour tortilla	53 gm (one 8 inch)	155

When you read the labeling on a food package, you'll notice that calories are based on a defined serving size, which may or may not accurately reflect normal consumption. For example, the labels on some 12-ounce cans of soft drinks list values based on two servings per can, although many people consume a whole can as a single serving.

Of course, we don't always eat equal weights of different foods. "Virtuously" eating reduced-fat and reduced-sugar foods will not necessarily lead to consuming fewer calories if you eat them in a greater volume! A boy who eats one tablespoon of peanut butter (about 45 calories) consumes fewer calories than a girl who eats a plain baked potato (about 140 calories). Even though peanut butter has more calories per gram than the baked potato, the potato weighs a lot more, and thus has more total calories than the peanut butter.

committing to physical activity, a student can achieve the ancient Greek ideal of a sound mind *and* a sound body. A balanced diet supports a healthy lifestyle by meeting the six fundamental nutritional needs to

1. ensure and maintain proper hydration and electrolyte balance,
2. develop and maintain an ideal body mass,
3. develop and preserve a lean body mass,
4. provide adequate carbohydrates to optimize metabolism,
5. maximize oxygen delivery, and
6. develop a high-density skeleton.

Ensure and Maintain Proper Hydration and Electrolyte Balance

It is important to maintain proper hydration and electrolyte balance, particularly during physical activity. Water constitutes 55 to 60 percent of an adult's body weight, and an even higher proportion of a child's weight. Sweating, vomiting, or urinating can cause dehydration. Conversely, excessive water intake can cause water intoxication.

The body attempts to maintain *homeostasis* (the proper level of hydration) by regulating both water intake and loss. When the concentration of *solutes* (which are dissolved chemicals, usually fairly simple compounds such as salt) in the blood is too high, receptors in the brain trigger the thirst sensation to make you want to drink. The brain regulates water loss through sweating, urination, and other mechanisms using similar signals.

While thirst signals the body's need for water, time-wise it lags behind that need. Dehydration leads to poor thermal regulation, loss of circulating water in the blood, and increased concentrations of sodium and potassium. Changes in electrolyte concentrations alter the performance of the heart and other neuromuscular systems. In addition, loss of circulating water in the blood reduces blood pressure. Students must know that they need to replenish lost water by drinking fluids (of any type) before, during, and after activity, rather than only when they become thirsty.

Although sweating causes a loss of salt along with water, people don't usually lose enough salt to require salt supplements. Americans take in plenty of salt through their diets. In fact, excessive salt consumption in some individuals can result in hypertension (high blood pressure) and other ailments, and is a serious public health problem.

Develop and Maintain an Ideal Body Mass

As children mature through the stages of life, they gain greater independence in creating a lifestyle. The choices that children make determine their ability to maintain an ideal *body mass*, which is defined as the sum of lean body tissue (primarily muscle and organs) and stored (depot) fat.

Physiological parameters that define an ideal body mass include growth, development, circulation, respiration capacity, and physical activity. For many years we have defined the ideal body mass by drawing on growth and activity tables from a large population, which figure them as a function of age, gender, and height. However, the Body Mass Index (BMI) is a more accurate measure of an individual's relative health. Population studies suggest that a BMI between 20 and 25 is ideal. A BMI lower than 20 indicates insufficient stores of body fat, which may reduce growth and activity. A BMI between 25 and 30, on the other hand, indicates overweight, and a BMI greater than 30 indicates obesity with a possibility of serious health impairment.

Obesity is now the biggest nutritional problem among youths. In our complex society, however, we cannot focus only on obesity. In fact, psychological and social

Females tend to have a greater percentage of body fat, with the ideal ranging from 18 to 23 percent body fat (compared with 16 to 19 percent for males). The body uses sexual hormones to regulate its body fat.

Determining Body Mass

Body Mass Index is the weight in kilograms (kg) divided by height in meters (m) squared (that is, kg/m^2). For example, a 145-pound (66-kilogram) adult who is 67 inches (1.7 meters) tall has a BMI of $66 / (1.7 \times 1.7) = 23$, which is in the "ideal" range.

Other ways to measure body fat include using convenient skinfold calipers (*FITNESSGRAM*); weighing the body underwater; and performing an isotope assay (the most accurate and expensive method). The BMI and caliper methods determine body composition quite accurately, and they are both convenient and inexpensive.

pressures to look thin have driven many youngsters to the extremes of anorexia and bulimia, which pose serious health risks. Helping your students achieve and maintain an ideal body mass requires teaching them the right combination of caloric intake, caloric expenditure, and behavior modification. Behavior modification includes the frequency of eating, the portion sizes of food, and commitment to physical activity.

Develop and Preserve a Lean Body Mass

Exercise both builds and breaks down muscle protein. Maintaining and increasing muscle mass requires optimal protein synthesis. Efficient production of new muscle mass results only when the diet provides all the amino acids, particularly the essential amino acids. A healthful diet includes enough high-quality protein to support muscle growth and sufficient energy sources to preserve amino acids for building muscle. This is particularly important during the growth years.

Provide Adequate Carbohydrates to Optimize Metabolism

In females very low body fat can limit the body's ability to produce female hormones, thus leading to brittle bones and osteoporosis—even in children. Maintaining an ideal body mass (ensuring that the body has enough fat) and performing weight-bearing activity to stimulate bone production will help prevent osteoporosis and brittle bones.

All dietary sugars, complex and simple, are metabolically equal. The body breaks down starches and sucrose into simple sugars for absorption. Sugar is both a fuel and an essential intermediate for burning fats and amino acids. For most individuals, young and old, the diet should supply enough carbohydrates to store glycogen in the muscles and liver as fuel for activity. However, excessive carbohydrate consumption can lead to weight gain, just as can excessive fat or protein consumption.

Maximize Oxygen Delivery

The diet must provide certain trace elements, particularly iron and copper, necessary to synthesize hemoglobin. In the red blood cells hemoglobin binds oxygen and carries it to the tissues. The rate of metabolism, and thus the generation of energy, is a direct function of oxygen utilization. Maximizing the delivery of oxygen to the red blood cells requires developing an optimal lung capacity for gas exchange. Physical activity greatly enhances the capacity of the lungs and the circulatory system's functioning.

Iron-deficiency anemia prevents the body from synthesizing hemoglobin. Anemia, therefore, is a special concern in students during their fast growth spurts. It also is important to avoid in early adolescence as girls approach menarche.

Develop a High-Density Skeleton

Throughout a life the body continuously builds and breaks down bone. Humans turn over their skeleton every 7 to 10 years. The bone is built from minerals (primarily calcium) and an organic matrix, much like reinforced concrete (see figure 7.3). Bone development depends on physical activity, nutrition, and heredity. Nutritional factors affecting bone density include calcium, vitamin D, and fluoride to build the mineral matrix and trace elements to build the collagen of the organic matrix. Dairy foods are the primary source of calcium for children and adolescents. The synthesis of bone is stimulated by weight-bearing exercises and hormone production.

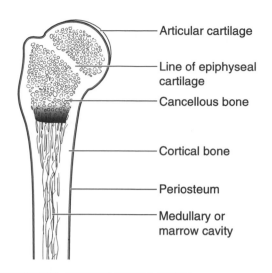

- Articular cartilage
- Line of epiphyseal cartilage
- Cancellous bone
- Cortical bone
- Periosteum
- Medullary or marrow cavity

Figure 7.3   Cross-section of the femur.

Biochemistry of Meeting the Six Fundamental Needs

The body is a complex chemical factory that takes raw material from the diet and the air and creates an astounding array of products—including the human body itself. The body needs different nutrients to meet each of its six fundamental needs. In this section, we'll look at how the body processes these nutrients.

Water and Electrolytes

Water is essential to life. No other substance is as widely involved in so many diverse functions. Water

- makes up slightly more than half of the normal body weight,
- transports nutrients throughout the circulatory system for delivery to cells and tissues,
- removes waste products by transporting them from cells and tissues through the circulatory system to the kidneys and then out of the body in the urine,
- plays an important role in the buffering system, which maintains the acid-alkaline balance in the body,
- is an important coolant as a temperature-regulation mechanism, and
- is involved as a reactant or solvent in almost every chemical reaction that occurs in the body.

Some beverages can actually lead to greater water loss. Caffeine (found in many soft drinks, tea, and coffee) and alcohol are both diuretics—that is, they cause the body to lose more water, usually through increased kidney function. Active people need to replenish their water, not lose even more.

Water may be bottled or delivered by tap. It comes also by way of milk and juices, which contain additional nutrients. Fruits, vegetables, and other foods as well contain water and nutrients. Water, however, is the most important nutrient. The body loses two to three quarts of water per day through normal activity—and even more with greater physical activity. Therefore, one must consume at least two to three quarts of various beverages and water daily to maintain adequate levels in the body. Humans can only survive four to five days without water.

Energy Sources and Building Blocks

Food provides the fuel for maintaining the energy-requiring processes that sustain life. We must constantly replenish energy reserves through nutrients that provide "burnable fuel": carbohydrates, fats, and proteins. Energy is measured in calories. Every calorie, no matter what the source, is equal.

The First and Second Laws of Thermodynamics show us the relationship between energy and nutrition. The First Law tells us that energy can neither be created nor destroyed. It can, however, be converted from one form to another. In nutritional terms, if energy is taken in as food and not used, it is stored as fat. The Second Law states that all systems in the universe have a tendency to become disorganized and chaotic. Preventing this chaos requires continuous energy expenditure. In nutritional terms, there are millions of cells in our body breaking down every second. Nutritional fuels provide the energy to repair, replace, and operate these cells.

Metabolism is a series of chemical reactions in which the body converts food to useful energy and heat, which it then uses to operate, build, and repair body tissues. Two processes work at the same time. One process, called *anabolism*, joins smaller molecules together to form larger molecules; it occurs, for example, in the growth and repair of cells and tissues. The other process, called *catabolism*, splits larger molecules into smaller molecules; it occurs, for example, when the body splits complex carbohydrates into simple sugars.

Metabolic Rates

Each individual has his or her own rate at which to convert the potential energy available in foodstuffs into stores of body energy. Through physical activity and proper nutrition a person can improve this rate of conversion: the *resting metabolic rate* (RMR)—or the amount of energy the body requires at rest to carry out such basic physiological functions as breathing, blood flow, and basal nerve and muscle activity. These functions alone consume 60 to 75 percent of the body's daily energy budget.

RMR varies with genetics, age, sex, physical activity level, and body type. Body type is determined by bone and muscle structure. A muscular person will have a higher RMR than a less muscular person of the same weight because muscle tissue requires more energy to maintain itself than does fat tissue.

Another consequence of the First Law of Thermodynamics is the need to take in building materials. Just as we can only change the form of energy, not create or destroy it, we can only change the form of matter, not create or destroy it. The matter forming the body must come from somewhere; that somewhere is the diet. The body uses nutrients in different ways as raw material for life's energy and structures, just as we might use wood to heat houses or build them.

Carbohydrates. Carbohydrates, both sugars and starches, are the body's principle source of energy. One gram of carbohydrate yields four calories (kilocalories). The body converts all sugars to glucose, the form of sugar that the cells use for energy. Glucose is the building block for other sugars (lactose, maltose, and galactose), amino acids, and nucleic acids.

The body stores any glucose it does not immediately use, since (under the First Law) it can't simply destroy the energy. It converts some of the glucose to glycogen and stores it in the liver and muscle; it converts the rest of the glucose to fat.

Dietary fibers are complex, indigestible carbohydrates that come from plants. *Insoluble* fiber absorbs water and helps provide the diet with needed bulk for the proper elimination of waste. *Soluble* fiber combines with waste substances to assist in their removal from the body.

Almost all foods, both natural and processed, contain carbohydrates. Grains, fruits, vegetables, and sweets, such as candies and baked goods, all contain both simple and complex carbohydrates to fuel the body. Whole grains and fruit or vegetable seeds and skins contain insoluble dietary fiber, whereas oat bran, apples, barley, beans, carrots, and other vegetables contain soluble fiber.

Proteins. The body uses protein both for fuel and as raw material for synthesizing tissues and hormones. Proteins are giant molecules consisting of chains of various of the 20 amino acids, strung together like beads. Protein synthesis requires the simultaneous presence of all 20 amino acids. The body can synthesize 10 of these amino acids, so they are termed *nonessential*. The other ten amino acids, called the *essential amino acids*, must come from the diet because the body is unable to make them. The breakdown and synthesis of protein is a normal function of the human body. As already mentioned, sugars are the primary fuel for the body. Proteins can be used for fuel if necessary. Proteins have the same caloric density as carbohydrates–that is, one gram of protein equals four calories.

The Sweet Things in Life

Although all cells require some glucose, the brain and nervous system rely almost completely on glucose for energy. The brain and nervous system use two-thirds of the glucose the body requires—about 500 calories a day. Although one can survive longer without carbohydrates than without water, feelings of hunger, sluggishness, and irritability set in when the glucose levels in the blood drop.

When carbohydrate intake is too low, the glucose and glycogen stores in the liver will be depleted within 24 hours. Although the body can use fat for two-thirds of its energy requirements, it cannot use fat directly for energy in the brain and nervous system. Furthermore, in the absence of sugar, the body breaks down fat into toxic ketone bodies, leading to *ketosis*. The body must look for other stores of glucose to help fuel the brain and nervous system; it breaks down protein sources in the body to make amino acids, which are converted in turn to sugars to prevent ketosis.

Based on a 2000-calorie daily diet, an adult needs between 250 and 300 grams of simple and complex carbohydrates each day to provide sufficient glucose. There are two types of carbohydrates. The simple sugars—glucose, fructose, sucrose, galactose, and lactose—are found primarily in fruits, vegetables, soft drinks, cakes, candies, and milk. The bloodstream rapidly transports these simple carbohydrates to body tissues. Starches are complex carbohydrates containing linked glucose molecules, and they occur in grains, grain products, and potatoes.

Dietary protein is broken down into amino acids, which are then absorbed into the blood stream. Each cell synthesizes the proteins it needs, including enzymes to facilitate and direct chemical reactions and key structural elements of the cell. The body also uses proteins as building blocks for antibodies (which protect the body from invading organisms), blood clots, hormones (such as insulin), and neurotransmitters. Finally, amino acids are precursors in the construction of the nucleic acids DNA and RNA.

The nutritional value of proteins depends on their complement of essential amino acids and their ease of digestion and absorption. Not all sources of proteins in the food supply are equal. A complete protein meal contains all the essential amino acids in the correct amounts required by the human body. Animal sources, such as poultry, meat, fish, eggs, and milk, provide complete proteins. Vegetable sources of protein, such as legumes and grains, are incomplete because (with the exception of soy protein) they don't provide all the essential amino acids. Vegetarians can obtain complete proteins (and still not eat animal products) by consuming legumes and grains together to create a complete protein.

Fats. Fats play important roles not only as fuel sources for the body, but also by adding pleasure, satiety (feeling of satisfaction), and taste to foods. The term

Kinds of Fats

Triglycerides, the most common form of fat, are composed of three long-chain, fatty acid hydrocarbon molecules joined to a glycerol. Like carbohydrates, fatty acids are composed of carbon, hydrogen, and oxygen. However, fatty acids have many more atoms of carbon and hydrogen in proportion to their oxygen, and so they supply more energy per gram. Few fatty acids that occur in foods or the body are free. Instead, they are usually found incorporated into trigylcerides. In the body, 99 percent of the stored body lipids are triglycerides.

There are two major types of fatty acids: saturated and unsaturated. Saturated fatty acids, found in shortening and animal fats, are usually solid at room temperature and contain the maximum number of hydrogen atoms per carbon atom; thus they have no double bonds. Unsaturated fatty acids contain one or more double bonds; they tend to remain liquid at room temperature and to come from plants. Oils such as olive and canola are rich in monounsaturated fatty acids, which have only one double bond. Polyunsaturated fatty acids, which are found in vegetable and some fish oils, contain more than one double bond. Margarine is a chemically saturated vegetable oil.

Stored body fat (triglycerides) provides a source of energy, thermal insulation, and protection from mechanical shock. Fatty acids serve as starting materials for important hormonal regulators. The phospholipids and sterols contribute to the cells' structures. Cholesterol serves as the raw material for steroid hormones, vitamin D, and bile. The lack of fat in the diet may lead to hair loss, abnormal skin conditions, failure to resist infection, and poor absorption of fat-soluble vitamins.

fat refers to all lipids: triglycerides (fats and oils), phospholipids (lecithin), and sterols (cholesterol). Fats are the most dense caloric energy source— one gram of fat equals nine calories.

Fats can be found in a wide variety of foods, in varying forms and amounts. Triglycerides in the diet deliver fat-soluble vitamins, bring flavor, aroma, and tenderness to foods, slow digestion, and contribute to a sense of satiety. Fats are found in foods of both plant and animal origin. They also are in processed sources, including breads, cakes, candy, dairy products, and cooking fats such as oils, shortening, and butter. In food, 95 percent of the lipids (triglycerides) are fats and oils, and the remaining 5 percent are such other lipids as phospholipids and sterols.

Only when fats are consumed in high quantities do they become a threat to an individual's health and well-being. Fats eaten with awareness and appreciation can bring pleasure to a meal. If eaten unconsciously and unnecessarily, however, they offer no such benefits. While eating special low-fat foods can, in theory, be beneficial for weight management, most people tend to eat *more* of these reduced fat foods, and may therefore fail to reduce their caloric intake.

Other Nutrients

Carbohydrates, proteins, and fats are the body's sources for energy for most of its structure. But these nutrients by themselves aren't enough. The body also needs vitamins and minerals to build chemical structures and to make and use energy.

Vitamins.   Vitamins are small organic molecules. After it was discovered that a deficiency of vitamins causes disease, they were determined to be essential substances. Only very small amounts of each vitamin are typically required in the diet. Vitamins differ from carbohydrates, fats, and proteins in many ways: They cannot be synthesized by our bodies, and must be obtained instead from the diet. Furthermore, some can be oxidized, or broken down, and rendered unable to perform their duties. Consequently, vitamins must be treated with respect in cooking and storing food.

We know enough about the structure and function of each vitamin to be able to synthesize all of them. Synthetic vitamins are identical in their activity to those

Table 7.1 Water-Soluble Vitamins

Vitamin	Functions	Sources
Thiamine (B$_1$)	Assists in energy metabolism; has a site on nerve-cell membrane to aid in muscle and tissue response.	Whole-grain foods
Niacin	Energy-transfer reactions and the metabolism of glucose, fat, and alcohol; oxidation-reduction reactions.	Milk, eggs, meat, poultry, fish, whole-grain and enriched breads and cereals
Riboflavin (B$_2$)	Coenzymes in energy metabolism; supports vision and skin health.	Milk, yogurt, cottage cheese, meat, green leafy vegetables, whole-grain bread and cereals.
Biotin	Part of coenzyme used in energy metabolism, fat synthesis, amino-acid metabolism, and glycogen synthesis.	Widespread in foods
Pantothenic acid	Energy metabolism.	Widespread in foods
Pyridoxal (B$_6$)	Helps make red blood cells; energy metabolism, amino-acid metabolism.	Green leafy vegetables, meats, fish, poultry, legumes, fruits, whole grains
Folate	New cell formation; nucleic-acid metabolism.	Green leafy vegetables, legumes, seeds, liver
B$_{12}$	New cell synthesis; maintains nerve cells; helps break down some fatty acids and amino acids.	Animal products (meat, fish, poultry, dairy, eggs)
Vitamin C	Collagen synthesis; antioxidant; amino-acid metabolism; absorption of iron.	Citrus fruits, cabbage-type vegetables, dark green vegetables, cantaloupe, strawberries, peppers, tomatoes, potatoes

of natural origin. The body converts all vitamins to either coenzymes, which assist enzymes with cell metabolism and energy production, or regulatory hormone-like molecules.

The nine water-soluble vitamins (see table 7.1) dissolve in water and cannot be stored in the body. Therefore, water-soluble vitamins need to be consumed more often than fat-soluble ones.

The four fat-soluble vitamins (see table 7.2) dissolve in fat and can be stored in the body. They are found in oils, greens, milk, and eggs. Given the proper precursors, the body can manufacture vitamins A and D. For example, the body

Table 7.2   Fat-Soluble Vitamins

Vitamin	Functions	Sources
Vitamin A	Vision, maintenance of the cornea, epithelial cells, mucous membranes; growth of skin, bone, and teeth.	Fortified milk, cheese, eggs, spinach, broccoli, orange fruits and vegetables
Vitamin D	Bone metabolism.	Sunlight, fortified milk, egg yolk, liver, fatty fish
Vitamin E	Antioxidant, stabilization of cell membranes.	Plant oils, green leafy vegetables, wheat germ, egg yolks
Vitamin K	Blood clotting; bone metabolism.	Liver, green leafy vegetables, milk

Table 7.3   Major Macrominerals

Macromineral	Functions	Sources
Calcium	Bone building; regulation of muscle activity; vision.	Milk products
Magnesium	Bone building; glucose utilization.	Nuts, avocados
Phosphorus	Bone building; cellular structure; cellular energy transfer.	Meat, fish, milk products
Sodium	Electrolyte balance; nerve and muscle function.	Salt
Potassium	Electrolyte balance; nerve and muscle function.	Bananas
Chloride	Electrolyte balance; nerve and muscle function.	Salt
Sulfur	Joint lubrication (in body-synthesized amino acids); allergic inflammation.	Meat, fish, milk products

can convert beta carotene, which is found in melons, squash, and carrots, to vitamin A. Sunlight on the skin helps transform cholesterol to vitamin D.

Minerals.   Minerals are inorganic elements that dissolve in water to become charged particles. Minerals cannot be changed and they keep their chemical identity. Nevertheless, they may be incorporated into proteins and other body structures. Minerals are involved in many aspects of the body's functioning. They are important in both electrolyte balance and acid-base balance. Nerve and muscle functioning depends critically on minerals, and many enzymes require minerals as a cofactor in order to function. So, too, the structure of many cells and tissues, particularly bone, relies on minerals.

The body requires the major minerals (*macrominerals*) in the largest amounts (see table 7.3). Minerals, except for calcium, are readily absorbed into the blood, freely transported, and rapidly excreted by the kidneys. As a result, the only mineral that the body stores is calcium; the others are quickly used or lost in waste products. Mineral-rich foods must be eaten regularly to replenish the body's supply.

Minerals are plentiful in the food supply, except for calcium and magnesium. Not enough people eat dairy products, which can supply 80 percent of the available calcium in a typical diet. Inadequate dietary calcium is the most common serious deficiency of minerals. While we must realize sodium's importance, too much sodium can lead to high blood pressure in some individuals.

Table 7.4   Trace Elements

Trace element	Functions	Sources
Iron	Hemoglobin protein; oxygen transport; respiration.	Red meats, fish, poultry, shellfish, eggs, legumes, dried fruits.
Zinc	Insulin; genetic material and proteins; immune reactions; transport of vitamin A; taste perception; wound healing; bone metabolism.	Protein-containing foods; meats, fish, grains, vegetables
Iodine	Thyroid hormone.	Seafood, bread, dairy products
Copper	Respiration; heme synthesis; collagen synthesis; bone metabolism.	Meats, shellfish, nuts
Manganese	Enzyme cofactors; bone and collagen.	Meats, nuts
Selenium	Oxidation-reduction, antioxidants, collagen.	Grains, seafood
Fluorine	Tooth and bone development.	Grains
Chromium	Maintains glucose homeostasis.	Meats, unrefined foods, fats, vegetable oils
Molybdenum	Facilitates (with enzymes) many cell processes.	Legumes, cereals, organ meats
Cobalt	Part of vitamin B_{12}; nerve formation and blood formation.	Meat, milk, dairy

Trace elements are also vital to one's health. They are the minerals (see table 7.4) that must be consumed in small amounts, hence they are called *microminerals*. There are 10 essential trace elements, the best known of which are iron, copper, zinc, iodine, and selenium. Trace elements, used as enzyme cofactors, are a crucial part of systems for oxygen transport, respiration, and the regulation of metabolism.

Consequences of Unhealthy Diets

We all want to believe in magic when it comes to nutrition and physical activity. Students must be taught, however, to separate magic and myth from reality. The belief that one can get something for nothing and achieve success without effort does not stand up to the First and Second Laws of Thermodynamics. No single diet or supplement is magical for losing or gaining weight, maintaining beautiful skin or hair, or imparting strength or agility.

Remembering the First Law of Thermodynamics, we can extend the principle to calories: all of them are equal, no matter what food source they come from. Consider some of the fashionable diets. Low-fat diets can provide pleasure in eating along with fewer fat calories. Consumed in large amounts, however, the reduced-fat items actually provide excessive calories. High-protein, moderate-fat, and low-carbohydrate diets suppress the appetite and lower calorie consumption, but such regimens may have toxic side effects. High-carbohydrate diets, which are low in fat and protein intake, restore carbohydrate depots for athletes, but this style of eating may compromise overall energy intake and provide too little protein.

If the diet provides inadequate levels of specific vitamins and minerals, nutritional supplements such as vitamin pills can make up the difference. There is little proof that supplementing the diet with vitamins and minerals *beyond* the RDA significantly benefits performance or enhances nutrition.

There are plenty of strategies you can use to help students learn good eating habits. Here are some underlying principles. Remember as you plan your activities with students that strategies for good eating should include these:

1. Individual eating habits should respect family lifestyles.
2. Begin the day with breakfast to provide energy and nutrients.
3. Control calorie consumption by spacing meals and snacks throughout the course of the day.

Dietary Disorders

Obesity (overweight) is an all-too-common consequence of poor lifestyle habits (Hill and Peters 1998). While some individuals may be genetically predisposed to becoming overweight, everyone can reduce their chance of obesity through a healthful diet and by increasing physical activity. Obesity results from one dietary factor alone: excessive caloric intake. Remember that all calories are equal. Those excess calories commonly come from eating too much fat, but they could come just as easily from simply eating too much (Taubes 1998). Obesity can have serious consequences, such as heart disease, diabetes, joint and bone injuries, and kidney disease. Limiting or eliminating excess weight is a matter of reducing the excessive caloric intake. The best way to reduce the excess is through a combination of healthier eating—consuming fewer calories—and greater physical activity, which burns off calories through both the activity itself and raising the RMR.

An obsession with overweight—or the perception of being overweight—can also result in serious harm, however. An individual who is seriously underweight is also unlikely to be fit. The most common eating disorders associated with underweight are anorexia and bulimia (Walsh and Devlin 1998). Advertising showing all body and dietary fat as "bad" only complicates the issue. Once again, a healthful diet, appropriate physical activity, and fitness knowledge are the best defenses against the eating disorders.

4. Find pleasure in food while being aware of its nutrient and caloric content.

5. Practice balance, variety, and moderation. Understand that there are no health foods and no junk foods.

6. Enjoy good food. Enjoy good health. Enjoy life.

Summary

The most serious consequence of an inadequate diet is an ongoing failure to achieve one's physical best. Diet provides both energy and building blocks for everyone, regardless of activity level. A fit individual eats a healthful diet. It's impossible to build aerobic endurance without having the energy to keep the heart rate elevated. Muscular strength and endurance require building new muscle tissue with nutrients. Good flexibility requires a healthy skeleton, also built from sufficient nutrient intake. And an ideal body composition clearly depends heavily on an appropriate diet. Good diet alone cannot create fitness; neither can activity alone.

In most school-based programs, the concepts of nutrition are taught in health or biology-related courses, while the concepts of physical activity are assigned to physical education classes. Both of these very important concepts must fit into our lives and the lives of our students as one integrated concept, especially since we are constantly bombarded with sound bites about nutrition and exercise information from marginally informed media sources and word-of-mouth.

PART II

Activities

Chapter 8
Aerobic Fitness

1 Skating Rink Aerobic Fun

Middle School Level

Warm-up is the beginning phase of the training session in which you prepare the body for activity. Proper warm-up improves the muscles' ability to perform work and helps prevent injuries by increasing blood flow, loosening and stretching muscle fibers and connective tissues (tendons and ligaments). **Cool-down** is gradually tapered back to a resting phase, after completing the cardiovascular phase of training. Proper cool-down reduces muscle soreness and allows muscles to flush wastes generated by exercise.

Purpose

Define warm-up and cool-down.

Equipment Needed

- Music tape
- Prepared movement cards

Relationship to National Standards

Physical Education Standard 3: Student exhibits a physically active lifestyle—Student participates regularly in health-enhancing physical activities to accomplish their goals in and out of the physical education class.

Health Education Standard 3: Student demonstrates the ability to practice health-enhancing behaviors and reduce health risks—Student demonstrates strategies to improve or maintain personal and family health.

Set Induction

Explain the importance of warm-up and cool-down. Ask students to provide a few examples of the greater flexibility of everyday objects (rubber bands, pasta, etc.) when warm than when cold.

Procedure

1. Students begin by walking in a large circle.
2. Using prepared cards, give students a new movement, such as those found at a roller or skating rink, each time they pass by.
3. Using activities such as ladies' choice jog, men's choice jog, coed groups of three jog, partner two-step shuffle, and so on, continue the movements until the students are adequately warmed up.

Teaching Hints

Use pauses in the music to stretch with students and explain the warm-up and cool-down benefits. Change directions of clockwise and counterclockwise. Allow students to warm up at their own level. Remind students that cooling down at the end of an exercise session by reversing this activity is equally important.

Closure and Assessment

Written and Oral

- Have students explain the benefits of a warm-up and cool-down.

Project

- Have students keep a fitness log of warm-up and cool-down routines for two weeks.

Extending the Lesson

Students create a warm-up and cool-down routine for an activity that they participate in regularly. They should include this in their fitness logs.

2 Aerobic Fitness Parcheesi

Middle School Level

Aerobic endurance is the ability of the body's energy systems to carry and use nutrients as fuels and building blocks over a given period of time. Fitness of the circulatory, respiratory, and muscular systems is especially important for good aerobic endurance.

Purpose

Students will be able to participate in a variety of continuous aerobic activities and to take their pulse rates at the carotid and radial arteries.

Equipment Needed

- Music tape for work and rest intervals
- Cards defining a variety of aerobic tasks
- 1 large six-sided die
- A variety of equipment depending on the aerobic tasks
- Poly-spots (either purchased or made)

Relationship to National Standards

Physical Education Standard 3: Student exhibits a physically active lifestyle—Student explores a variety of new physical activities for personal interest, in and out of physical education class.

Health Education Standard 3: Student demonstrates the ability to practice health-enhancing behaviors and reduce health risks—Student demonstrates strategies to improve or maintain personal and family health.

Set Induction

Define aerobic endurance. Ensure that students understand that we determine whether an activity is aerobic by measuring pulse, breathing, or sweating. Review taking a pulse over the heart, at the carotid (neck) artery, and at the radial (wrist) artery. Although this activity concentrates on pulse, remind the students to think about their breathing and sweating after each activity.

Procedure

1. Set up four cones at the corners of the playing area and put different colored poly-spots between the cones to connect them, making a game board. Students will roll the large die to see how many poly-spots they move during the game. Place a card with an aerobic activity listed on it under each spot. Activities might include jumping rope forward and backward, step aerobics, basketball dribbling, soccer dribbling, power walking, swim jogging, stride jumping, boxer stepping, volleyball jumping and spiking, and others appropriate to the space available. Make one or more poly-spots a "free" area, where students choose fun activities to do, such as hula hoops, line dancing, or making up their own physical activity. You can use these "free" areas to help ensure that there is adequate space for the other activities.

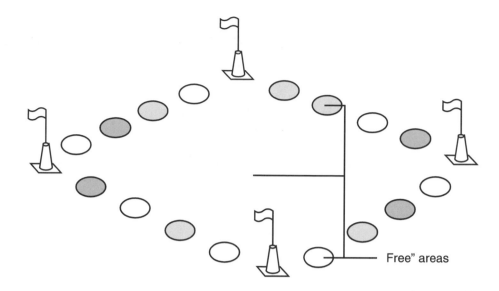

Free" areas

2. To begin the game, have the students stand on a poly-spot. On your signal the students look at the activity card under their spots and perform the activity listed on that card. They continue until they hear the stop signal or the music stops.
3. Students roll the die again, and they all move either clockwise or counterclockwise that number of poly-spots on the "game board." They look under their new spot and begin that new activity upon hearing the signal.
4. Students will take their pulse rates after completing an aerobic task.

Teaching Hints

Working in pairs may be an option, too. Make the inside rectangle a free area, where students choose activities from the available equipment. After a discussion about aerobic endurance, allow students to create a card for the game board. Use a prepared tape with 60-second work to 15-second rest intervals. Teach the students how to find their radial and carotid arteries. They can take their heart rates at various times during the game for six seconds.

Closure and Assessment

Written and Oral
- Have students identify and write a definition for aerobic endurance.
- Have students list three favorite activities from this game that were aerobic. Ask them how they knew these activities were aerobic.

Project
- Have students record their pulses on a worksheet after each activity.

Extending the Lesson

- Students prepare a log of heart rates for various activities at home, such as raking leaves, vacuuming, riding a bike, and so on.
- Students research four different activities for aerobic endurance: team and individual sports, recreational games, outdoor activities, and occupations or work. They compare heart rates of people performing the activity, for example, playing soccer, wrestling, hiking, cleaning the house, and doing office work.

3 Aerobic Benefit Circuit

Middle School Level

Improving **aerobic endurance** increases the ability of the heart, lungs, and muscles to do work over a longer period of time. Together, good nutrition and physical activity will promote lifelong health benefits and disease prevention. To feel good and enjoy life, physical activity and nutrition should be fun, individual, and pleasurable.

Purpose

Students will understand the health benefits of aerobic endurance and be able to rank the benefits to meet personal needs and goals.

Equipment Needed

- Stopwatch
- Music
- Task sheets
- Health benefits signs for each station (e.g., benefits of step benches, cone run, jump rope, ski jump, stair climb, agility run, dribble through cones, hot shot)

Relationship to National Standards

Physical Education Standard 3: Student exhibits a physically active lifestyle—Student identifies the benefits from regular physical activity.

Health Education Standard 3: Student demonstrates the ability to practice health-enhancing behaviors and reduce health risks—Student demonstrates strategies to improve or maintain personal and family health.

Set Induction

Ask students why aerobic endurance is important to good health. Brainstorm a list of diseases that can be reduced by regular aerobic activity. Explain that today's activity will give students information to help choose which benefits are most important to them.

Procedure

1. Develop an aerobic activity circuit with 8 to 10 stations that teach the benefits of aerobic endurance. Items for aerobic endurance health benefits cards could include:
   - reduce illness—jump rope
   - reduce stress—bench step
   - improve appearance—agility run
   - reduce risk of heart disease—cone run
   - control weight—ski jump
   - increase enjoyment of life—cone dribble
   - have more energy—stair climb
   - increase self-discipline—speed jump

2. When the music starts, students will walk or jog laps around the gym for 15 to 30 seconds. When the music stops, the students choose a health benefit station, read the health benefit, and perform the activity at the station for 60 seconds. When the music begins, the students repeat the walking or jogging, then rotate to another health benefit station and perform the activity.

3. The activity continues until the students perform the number of station choices you decide.

4. At the end of the activity, students record their choices and discuss why they chose those benefits, either in a journal or in class.

Teaching Hints

Start students at several spots before they jog. You can use task sheets or not depending on the number of stations the students choose. If too many students choose one station, they can simulate the activity or share the equipment at the station. The important concept is not the workout, but the health benefit choices they make.

Closure and Assessment

Written and Oral

• In a journal, have the students list five personal benefits from participating in aerobic activity, and explain which three are most important to them and why.

Project

• Encourage students to participate in some form of physical activity after their next stressful situation. Have them describe in their journals the feelings during and after this stressful experience and whether exercise helped them feel lower stress.

Extending the Lesson

• Students develop a timeline prioritizing their health risks. Ask them if their benefits might change in priority over the years, and what things (other than just age) might cause any such changes.

• Students list the heart attack risk factors and how activity affects each. Determine which risk factors are controllable and which are not.

| **4** | **Frequency Star** | |

Middle School Level

Frequency is how often you do your chosen aerobic activity. You should do aerobic activity most days of the week, accumulating at least 30 minutes each day.

Purpose

Students will learn that they should be active most days a week based on their chosen aerobic activity.

Equipment Needed

- Mats
- Day off cards
- Five-star fitness signs
- Necessary equipment for the five points

Relationship to National Standards

Physical Education Standard 3: Student exhibits a physically active lifestyle—Student regularly participates in physical activity to develop a healthy lifestyle.

Health Education Standard 3: Student demonstrates the ability to practice health-enhancing behaviors and reduce health risks—Student demonstrates strategies to improve or maintain personal and family health.

Set Induction

Bring a copy of the Surgeon General's *Report* to class. Explain that it provides important guidelines to follow to achieve optimal health. Explain that today's activity will help students understand the recommended frequency of aerobic activity.

Procedure

1. Explain that the points on the star represent five days of the week. As students travel from point to point (day to day), they perform an aerobic activity at each stop. One layout might be:
   - Step aerobics
   - Swim jogging
   - Basketball dribbling
   - Jumping rope
   - Jogging the star pattern and encouraging others to do their best
2. The travel pathway tracks a star pattern. Students will move from point to point on your cue. One-fifth of the class starts at each point.
3. Keep students at each point for 1-2 minutes, depending on the tasks you choose.

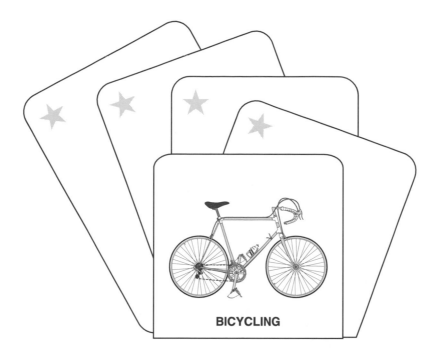

BICYCLING

Teaching Hints

You may want to identify a safe base (a mat) in the middle as a day off area. Students can access the mat area as they travel from one point to another. Students may go there during one rotation to reinforce the idea that not everyone will choose to be active every day of the week. Establish a specific rotation order for the different stations, including the "day off" area. Encourage students to think about including aerobic activity on weekend days, especially if it is not possible to schedule activity every school day.

Closure and Assessment

Written and Oral

- After participating in the activity, have students list and illustrate one aerobic activity they could participate in alone, with a friend, with their families, in the community, and at school.

Project

- Have students prepare a one-month calendar of aerobic activities illustrating how they would meet the criteria of frequency by participating in activities that they can do alone, with a friend, in the community, at school, and with their families.

Extending the Lesson

After one month, have students review their one-month calendars and note how successful they were in including frequent aerobic activity. Repeat the calendar creation and have the students record the actual activities performed for this month.

5 | Heartbeat Stations

Middle School Level

Intensity is the level at which you perform an activity, ranging from moderate to vigorous. Intensity for aerobic activity can be correlated with heart rate, which can indicate oxygen use and respiration activity. The intensity you need to improve or maintain your aerobic endurance depends on the type of activity you choose.

Purpose

Students will participate in a variety of activities to understand how physical activity at varying intensity levels influences the heart rate and perceived exertion.

Equipment Needed

- Heart rate monitors (if available)
- Score sheets and pencils
- Stopwatch

Relationship to National Standards

Physical Education Standard 4: Student achieves and maintains a health-enhancing level of fitness—Student monitors intensity of exercise.

Health Education Standard 3: Student demonstrates the ability to practice health-enhancing behaviors and reduce health risks—Student demonstrates strategies to improve or maintain personal and family health.

Set Induction

Define intensity. Ask students to predict which aerobic endurance activities have greater intensity and explain why.

Procedure

1. Set up an aerobic endurance circuit with activities that vary in intensity: walking through cones, jumping rope, jogging around the gym, dribbling a soccer ball, running the agility ladder, and so on.
2. As a warm-up, students will participate in six activities—sitting, standing, walking, power walking, jogging, and sprinting—for 30 seconds each, resting for 30 seconds between activities.
3. Upon completing each station, students will measure their pulses, either with the heart rate monitors or by counting for six seconds and adding zero to the number.
4. Ask the students to identify the station where their hearts beat the fastest and slowest and explain why.

Teaching Hints

Because this activity is vigorous, you may want to include muscular strength sports skills that produce aerobic endurance or other endurance activities in this circuit. Other activities can be shooting hoops, dribbling the soccer ball through cones, and so on. Provide paper and pencils for recording the heart rate after each activity.

Closure and Assessment

Written and Oral

- Have each student explain which of their predictions of intensity from the set induction were correct and why.

Project

- Have students look at a range of magazines promoting different kinds of activities that they do not do. Have the students describe the activity, predict the activity's intensity, and explain their prediction.

Extending the Lesson

Discuss the results with the class and have each student record his or her results. After a training period of two to three weeks, the students may repeat the activity on their own and compare results. Ask them to explain how to modify the activity so that their intensity now (measured by heart rate) will match what they recorded at the beginning of the training period.

6 | 10-Minute Ticker Tasks

Middle School Level

Time is how long you need to be aerobically active to improve or maintain aerobic endurance. You should accumulate at least 30 minutes of aerobic activity most days of the week.

Purpose

Students will understand that an increase of time in aerobic activity maintains or improves aerobic endurance. Research shows that 10-minute bouts of aerobic activity are beneficial, and students should work to accumulate at least 30 minutes a day.

Equipment Needed

- Depends on the activities you choose

Relationship to National Standards

Physical Education Standard 4: Student achieves and maintains a health-enhancing level of physical fitness—Student understands and applies training principles to improve physical fitness.

Health Education Standard 3: Student demonstrates the ability to practice health-enhancing behaviors and reduce health risks—Student demonstrates strategies to improve or maintain personal and family health.

Set Induction

Discuss the relationship between time and intensity. Explain that intensity is measured throughout an activity, while the time is measured only at the end.

Procedure

1. Design a variety of motivational aerobic fitness tasks to meet the needs and interests of your students. Include 10-minute tickers as a way to begin or end a lesson. This could be a weekly event to measure aerobic fitness improvements. If heart rate monitors are available, use them during this activity. Here are some examples of 10-minute ticker tasks:

   - Using the steps, students choose 10 different movements and perform each for 1 minute.
   - Students play 1-on-1 or 2-on-2 basketball and check their heart rates three times during the game.
   - Students practice their favorite hip hop, country swing, or aerobic dance with their friends.
   - Using the jump rope, students check their skills with a skill sheet.
   - Students jog the track and pass a football to a partner. They take turns running pass patterns.

2. Have students keep a fitness journal or log of accomplishments to measure and evaluate improvements.

Teaching Hints

This is an excellent way to allow students to choose a task and experience individual successes. It allows total inclusion of a variety of developmental levels. Make sure to include a warm-up and cool-down with this activity.

Closure and Assessment

Written and Oral

- Have students explain how to accumulate different activities to meet the 30-minute goal.

Project

- Have students create a one-week aerobic fitness plan based on accumulating fitness activities in 10-minute segments. Ensure that the plans include a variety of activities.

Extending the Lesson

Students develop a list of 10-minute tickers to perform at home with their families. They write in their journals a log of 10-minute ticker activities for three weeks, including activities such as mowing the lawn, shoveling snow, dancing to music, and so on. Students measure resting heart rate, target heart rate, and recovery heart rate during each activity.

7 Aerobic Condition Circuit

Middle School Level

Type means what specific activity you participate in to improve or maintain your aerobic endurance.

Purpose

Students will understand how to choose what type of activities will improve or maintain aerobic endurance levels.

Equipment Needed

- Aerobic conditioning circuit signs
- Music tape
- Equipment for circuit activities

Relationship to National Standards

Physical Education Standard 3: Student exhibits a physically active lifestyle—Student explores a variety of new physical activities for personal interest in and out of the physical education class.

Health Education Standard 3: Student demonstrates the ability to practice health-enhancing behaviors and reduce health risks—Student demonstrates strategies to improve or maintain personal and family health.

Set Induction

Define specificity. Ask students to state and discuss examples of activities designed to improve aerobic endurance.

Procedure

1. Set up a variety of aerobic conditioning stations for various sports, such as shadow boxing, step, jump rope, football carioca, basketball agility run, free choice, swimming, soccer dribbling, personal conditioning (walk, jog, step), and so on.

2. Use a segmented music tape. Students will participate in each activity for 30 to 45 seconds while the music plays. They rotate to the next station when the music is off.

3. Continue until the students have completed all stations.

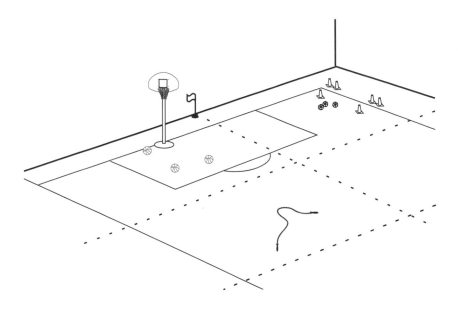

Teaching Hints

Have students practice each activity before beginning the circuit. Because this circuit is vigorous, you may want to stop halfway and include muscular endurance and flexibility exercises. Explain to the students that there are a variety of activities and sports that have aerobic benefits. Participating in aerobic activities and sports inside and outside of school will benefit the heart, lungs, and muscles.

Closure and Assessment

Written and Oral

- Have students state how each station is specific to improving aerobic endurance.

Project

- Have students examine one station's activity. How does that activity specifically improve each of the elements of health-related fitness?

Extending the Lesson

Over a week, have students participate in a variety of activities, such as aerobics, sports, and household chores, and take their pulse counts for each activity. Have students write in their journals how each activity may or may not contribute to cardiovascular endurance development.

8   Making Progress

Middle School Level

Overload is an increase in frequency, intensity, or time beyond the body's normal capacity. Levels of overload should be based upon an individual's fitness goals. Overload for aerobic endurance requires increasing heart rate within the training zone, exercising for longer, or both. The concepts of **frequency, intensity, time**, and **type or specificity** (FITT) offer knowledge to choose strategies for doing more, which leads to demonstrating **progression**.

Purpose

The student demonstrates progression from baseline fitness performance toward a realistic goal that he or she selects, with support as needed from the teacher.

Equipment Needed

- PACER tape
- Measured area of 20 meters (21 yards, 32 inches) or running area equal to 1 mile

Relationship to National Standards

Physical Education Standard 4: Student achieves and maintains a health-enhancing level of physical fitness—Student meets the health-related fitness standards as defined by *FITNESSGRAM*.

Health Education Standard 3: Student demonstrates the ability to practice health-enhancing behaviors and reduce health risks—Student demonstrates strategies to improve or maintain personal and family health.

Set Induction

Discuss the need for both short- and long-term goals. Explain and provide examples of the goal-setting process.

Procedure

1. Select an assessment strategy to establish students' baseline aerobic endurance. Choices from the *FITNESSGRAM* include PACER and a one-mile run or walk.
2. Students perform the assessments.
3. Discuss the goal-setting process with the class.
   - Students set their goals (for example, identify an improved score).
   - Students choose their strategies (teacher can supply strategies or students can brainstorm).
   - Students record their plans (see sample forms in the appendix).
4. Students follow their plans.
5. Reassess and look for progress in students' performance. Remind them to respect the efforts of others and to keep scores confidential. Examples include:
   - A formal, individualized *FITNESSGRAM* report
   - A chart of standards for students to examine on their own

Teaching Hints

Be aware that comparing and proving self is common at this age. Remind students to respect others' feelings and the confidentiality of assessment scores.

Closure and Assessment

Written and Oral

• Create *FITNESSGRAM* reports.

Project

• Individuals prepare a student assessment record independently, using a standards chart such as that included with *FITNESSGRAM*.

Extending the Lesson

• Students create a calendar, a graph, or write in their journals recording progress toward their goals.

• Repeat the goal-setting part of this activity after six weeks. Help the students understand that goals will change over time.

9   Jump, Step, Jog

Middle School Level

Progression is a sequential change in frequency, intensity, and/or time. **Overload** is an increase in frequency, intensity, or time beyond the body's normal capacity. Levels of overload should be based upon an individual's fitness goals.

Purpose

Students will identify one fitness principle that they can alter to demonstrate progression.

Equipment Needed

- Jump ropes
- Steps
- Music tape

Relationship to National Standards

Physical Education Standard 4: Student achieves and maintains a health-enhancing level of physical fitness—Student understands and applies training principles to improve physical fitness.

Health Education Standard 3: Student demonstrates the ability to practice health-enhancing behaviors and reduce health risks—Student demonstrates strategies to improve or maintain personal and family health.

Set Induction

Define progression. Discuss how progression relates to intensity, specificity, and time. Explain that this lesson will show progression over a short period, although progression actually occurs over a longer period.

Procedure

1. Students work in groups of three. One student will jog, another will jump rope, and the third will perform step aerobics.
2. Use a segmented music tape (30:10 seconds). When the music is on, students perform their aerobic activity. When the music stops, students rotate to the next activity.
3. Continue until they have participated in all three aerobic activities.
4. On day two, use a 40:10 second music tape to increase the time students participate in aerobic activities.

Teaching Hints

On day one, have students work in groups of three. On day two, students can choose the aerobic activities they wish to participate in. Brainstorm with students about what other activities they can include in the circuit. Include some of their activities in the circuit the rest of the week.

Closure and Assessment

Written and Oral

- Students identify and write a definition for overload.
- Students identify and write a definition for progression.

Project

- Students choose an activity they would enjoy participating in to keep the heart, lungs, and muscles fit. Using this activity, students develop a list of ways to work harder and do a little more each exercise episode.
- Explain how students can demonstrate the concept of progression for each exercise in the jump, step, jog activity.

Extending the Lesson

Given three scenarios (e.g., Susie's, Sam's, and Sarah's story), have students design strategies for each that will result in progression.

- Susie's story: Susie has asthma, but can do limited aerobic activity. Her baseline is 3 minutes of activity on the PACER. She wants to improve to 5 minutes.
- Sam's story: Sam is on the basketball team. He wants to play longer without getting so tired.
- Sarah's story: Sarah can run one-quarter mile without stopping. She wants to run one mile without stopping.

10 | Warm-Up/Cool-Down

High School Level

Warm-up is the beginning phase of the training session in which you prepare the body for activity. Proper warm-up helps prevent injuries by loosening and stretching muscle fibers and connective tissues (tendons and ligaments). **Cool-down** is gradually tapering back, almost to a resting phase, after completing the cardiovascular phase of training. Proper cool-down helps prevent injuries by allowing muscles to flush wastes generated by exercise.

Purpose

The students will learn how warm-up and cool-down activities affect the heart rate. They will learn how important it is to keep moving after moderate-to-vigorous activity to prevent blood from pooling in the extremities.

Equipment Needed

- Stopwatch
- Paper and pen or pencil for each student

Relationship to National Standards

Physical Education Standard 4: Student achieves and maintains a health-enhancing level of physical fitness—Student designs a personal fitness program.

Health Education Standard 3: Student demonstrates the ability to practice health-enhancing behaviors and reduce health risks—Student demonstrates strategies to improve or maintain personal and family health.

Set Induction

Review the need for a complete warm-up prior to exercise. Explain that the heart is a muscle that also needs to be warmed up.

Procedure

1. Students develop a workout plan for improving their aerobic endurance based on their needs and goals. The plan should include both a warm-up and a cool-down.
2. Students then test their workout plans. They will record their heart rates after each step in the plan, including the warm-up and cool-down.

Teaching Hints

To demonstrate the effects of not cooling down, have the students immediately sit down while taking their 1-minute heart rate. Do not use a 6-, 10-, or 15-second count for the heart rate, because the best way to see the results of a cool-down is to take a 1-minute heart rate.

Closure and Assessment

Written and Oral

• Have students distinguish among the heart rate at rest, during warm-up, and during aerobic activity.

Project

• Have students record the data of their 1-minute heart rates from participating in warm-up and cool-down activities for several days.

Extending the Lesson

Have the students compare their recorded warm-up and cool-down heart rates over several weeks. Is there any difference?

11 Walk, Jog, Sprint

High School Level

Aerobic endurance is the ability of the body's energy systems to carry and use nutrients as fuels. Fitness of the circulatory, respiratory, and muscular systems is especially important for good aerobic endurance.

Purpose

Students will understand that varying aerobic activities will increase their heart and breathing rates. They will learn to calculate and monitor their aerobic training heart values.

Equipment Needed

- Fast-paced music
- Score cards
- Stopwatches

Relationship to National Standards

Physical Education Standard 4: Student achieves and maintains a health-enhancing level of activity—Student engages in sustained activity, causing increased heart and breathing rates.

Health Education Standard 3: Student demonstrates the ability to practice health-enhancing behaviors and reduce health risks—Student develops strategies to improve or maintain personal, family, and community health.

Set Induction

Review the function of the heart muscle. You may want to use a hand water pump to pump water first slowly, then faster, to demonstrate increased circulation with faster pumping.

Procedure

1. Have students walk for about 400 meters (one lap around a quarter-mile track) and record their 15-second pulses.
2. Next, have the students jog 400 meters and record their 15-second pulses.
3. Finally, have the students then run hard for 400 meters and record their 15-second pulses.
4. Students will calculate their aerobic training heart values. Each student should compare the heart and breathing rates of the different activities to determine which one was most effective for his or her health.

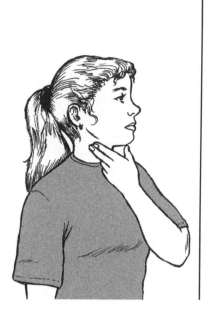

Teaching Hints

Start the activity with the students finding their resting heart rate, then calculating their target heart rate zone. Have students practice using the different formulas. If you do not have a track to perform this activity, you could set up an oval or rectangle with cones. Use music to enhance this activity. Students can count their breathing rates and describe perspiration levels. **Safety Note:** If any students reach the top level of training heart rate at a walk or jog, do not ask them to perform step 3.

Closure and Assessment

Written and Oral

- Have the students describe their own aerobic fitness level based on how closely they approached the top level of the training heart rate while sprinting.

Project

- Students will graph the effects of each activity (walk, jog, and sprint) on their heart rates, breathing, and perspiration. They will use this information to write a brief paragraph about the influence each activity has on aerobic endurance. This assessment depends on accurately determining resting and target heart rates and comparing the effects of the three activities on developing aerobic endurance.

Extending the Lesson

Students log heart rates for various activities at home that they might use for developing the aerobic system. They should then explain how each of these activities would develop the aerobic system.

12   Aerobic Experiment

High School Level

Aerobic endurance and a **healthful diet** are necessary for optimal health and performance. Aerobic exercise helps maintain efficient and proper function of the cardiovascular and respiratory systems. A healthful diet provides necessary nutrients to sustain energy levels and allow efficient functioning of body systems. Active lifestyles and different life stages change the body's nutritional demands.

Purpose

Students will choose an aerobic activity to receive health benefits based on their individual needs and interests. They will also select an activity to meet the general needs of one other age group (younger or older than themselves).

Equipment Needed

- Videos, TV, or VCR
- Hand weights
- Stopwatch

Relationship to National Standards

Physical Education Standard 3: Student exhibits a physically active lifestyle—Student seeks and selects physical activities from a variety of movement forms based on personal interest, meaning, and fulfillment.

Health Education Standard 3: Student demonstrates the ability to practice health-enhancing behaviors and reduce health risks—Student develops strategies to improve or maintain personal, family, and community health.

Set Induction

Review the difference between resting and working heart rates. Brainstorm differences which could be related to nutrition and body composition.

Procedure

1. Have the students write a short paragraph on what they need to do to improve their current aerobic health status. Then they can complete one of the following activities each day for one week:
   - Do a 40-minute leisure walk.
   - Do a 30-minute power walk with hand weights.
   - Do a 15- to 20-minute walk or jog.
   - Complete a 30-minute aerobic program or video.
   - Complete a 40-minute step aerobic program or video.
2. Have the students record their 1-minute exercise heart rates at the end of each of the five activities.
3. Students will then write a paragraph on how they felt physically (muscles tired, hunger, overall tiredness) and mentally (reduced stress, refreshed, energetic) after completing each activity.

Day	Activity	Pulse
Monday	Walk	
Tuesday	Walk w/weights	
Wednesday	Walk/jog	
Thursday	Aerobic	
Friday	Step aerobic	

4. Finally, have each student compare which activities best met their health benefit needs.

Teaching Hints

Prepare a recording chart and handouts (see appendix for base values). You may use options other than the activities listed previously, for example, the bike, treadmill, StairMaster, or after-school sports, such as basketball practice. This is particularly necessary for inclusion and for students with significant fitness deficits.

Closure and Assessment

Written and Oral

• Have each student state one personal characteristic that affects aerobic endurance, and briefly describe how to alter that characteristic to improve aerobic endurance (if it can be altered).

Project

• Students will record personal health data from participating in five different aerobic activities and evaluate the appropriateness of each activity in their personal fitness plan.

Extending the Lesson

Students design and conduct an interview survey and compare health status (as described by the individual) and level of physical activity in the following age groups: 15 to 20, 21 to 35, 36 to 55, 56 to 75, and 76 to 90. Students determine the relationship between physical activity and perceived health of the people they interviewed.

13 Student Frequency Log

High School Level

Frequency is how many days a week you perform aerobic activity. You should do some form of activity most days of the week, accumulating at least 30 minutes each day. Frequent activity maintains efficiency of heart, lungs, and blood vessels to enhance the circulation of oxygen to the cells.

Purpose

Students will understand that their choices of activities and personal goals will influence the frequency and intensity of their aerobic activity and its potential to achieve a healthful level of fitness.

Equipment Needed

- Worksheet in appendix

Relationship to National Standards

Physical Education Standard 3: Student exhibits a physically active lifestyle. Student participates regularly in health-enhancing and personally rewarding physical activity outside the physical education class—Student selects physical activities from a variety of movement forms based on personal interest, meaning, and fulfillment.

Health Education Standard 3: Student demonstrates the ability to practice health-enhancing behaviors and reduce health risks—Student demonstrates strategies to improve or maintain personal and family health.

Set Induction

Review the goal-setting process, the FITT factors, and age-appropriate *FITNESSGRAM* standards. Remind students that reaching and maintaining the standards depends on progress over time, not performance on a single assessment.

Procedure

1. Using the form in the appendix as a guide, students will record the number of activity points they earn each day. Students should earn at least two points per day and record their activity for three to six weeks.

2. Encourage the students to try a variety of exercises to meet their personal health goals. Focus on encouraging students to try exercises they've never tried before.

Teaching Hints

Students perform this activity outside the physical education class. Explain that they should carry out the intense activities (greater point values) on alternate days to prevent injuries and fatigue. For example, they could do walking daily, but do running on alternate days until they start to feel comfortable doing this activity daily.

Closure and Assessment

Written and Oral

- Ask students which activities they would choose if they could work out only three days a week. Have the students describe how are these different from a five- or seven-day workout plan.

Project

- Students maintain a record of participation, indicating frequency, perceived intensity, and relationship to desired benefits.

Extending the Lesson

Have the students set a personal health goal for aerobic endurance in one or two of their favorite aerobic activities by changing the frequency of their workouts. They can keep a log indicating the number of days a week they performed the activity, how they felt, and who they worked out with.

14 Aerobics Pentathlon

High School Level

Intensity refers to the level at which you must work to reach your target heart rate. The aerobic activity you choose influences the intensity you need to meet your personal goals. Your current fitness status, personal goals, physical skills, time, and other life responsibilities are factors that influence the activities you choose. Many activities provide aerobic benefit but at varying intensities. Intensity relates to frequency, duration, and the type of activity you choose. You perceive exertion through increases in heart rate, breathing, perspiration, and tiredness.

Purpose

Students will learn when an activity intensity reaches the aerobic training effort by calculating their heart rates and measuring their perceived exertion. To calculate the target heart rate zone, students will use one of several formulas. The students will participate in a variety of activities at varying intensities.

Equipment Needed

- Stopwatch
- Recording sheets

Relationship to National Standards

Physical Education Standard 4: Student achieves and maintains a health-enhancing level of physical fitness—Student demonstrates the skill, knowledge, and desire to monitor and adjust activity levels to meet personal fitness needs.

Health Education Standard 3: Student demonstrates the ability to practice health-enhancing behaviors and reduce health risks—Student demonstrates strategies to improve or maintain personal and family health.

Set Induction

Review the FITT principles, emphasizing individual differences. Discuss how individual fitness levels will affect the appropriate intensity for aerobic endurance exercises.

Procedure

1. Set up five aerobic stations using sports games, drills, skills, dances, and individual activities or hobbies, such as biking, jogging, or walking.
2. Students will rotate through the stations and participate in a variety of activities that vary in intensity.
3. Have students record their heart rates based on a six-second count and their perceived exertion number on the Borg scale (see the appendix).

Teaching Hints

Have students bring calculators to class to calculate the target heart rates. They can practice calculating their target heart rate zones using each formula. Use heart rate monitors for students who are having difficulty finding their pulses. Explain perceived exertion rates and how the numbers correlate to their heart rates. Have a perceived exertion rate chart posted so they can compare their feelings with a number. Students can integrate aerobic endurance and body composition activities by comparing heart rate and calories used.

Closure and Assessment

Written and Oral

- Have students state what factors influenced their perception of exertion when there was a difference between the heart rate and perception of exertion.

Project

- Students will keep a log, recording actual and perceived heart rates after 5 minutes of participating in each of five selected aerobic activities. Students should perform the activities within their target heart rate zones. Then they can analyze the data to determine which activities have the greatest potential benefit.

Extending the Lesson

Students wear a heart rate monitor while participating in a variety of daily activities (include school, work, and household chores). They list the perceived heart rate and compare it with the actual heart rate.

15 Aerobic Endurance Time

High School Level

Time is defined as how long (duration) you do aerobic activity to improve or maintain fitness levels.

Purpose

Students will understand that time is a variable of overload (frequency, intensity, time, type). You should accumulate time during a 30-minute period, or in 10-minute bouts of activity that add up to 30 minutes, most days of the week.

Equipment Needed

- Summary table from the Surgeon General's *Report on Physical Activity and Health At-a-Glance* (appendix).

Relationship to National Standards

Physical Education Standard 4: Student achieves and maintains a health-enhancing level of physical fitness—Student demonstrates the skill, knowledge, and desire to monitor and adjust activity levels to meet personal fitness needs.

Health Education Standard 3: Student demonstrates the ability to practice health-enhancing behaviors and reduce health risks—Student demonstrates strategies to improve or maintain personal and family health.

Set Induction

Review the FITT principles. Discuss how time and intensity work together to create overload. Remind the students that improving fitness requires controlled overload.

Procedure

1. On a chalkboard, overhead, or handout list the following activities:
   - Dancing fast—30 minutes
   - Playing volleyball—45 minutes
   - Running at 10-minute-mile pace—15 minutes
   - Raking leaves—30 minutes
2. Have the students choose and participate in at least one of the activities listed.
3. Have students match the recommended time for each activity with the Surgeon General's recommendations for healthy activities.
4. Hand out a copy of the summary table from the Surgeon General's *Report* (see appendix). The answers to the matching activity are found in this report.

Teaching Hints

The purpose of this lesson is to discover how duration of participation relates to intensity, frequency, and calories used, as well as to the type of activity and its desired benefit. The Surgeon General's *Report* indicates it is important to perform aerobic activity a total of 30 minutes most days of the week, either in short bouts or all together. Explain that the exact time required to improve aerobic endurance depends on the type of activity chosen and personal goals. Students can integrate aerobic endurance and body composition activities by comparing time and calories used.

Closure and Assessment

Written and Oral

- Students select three of their favorite activities and write a brief description about the relationship among time, type of activity, and potential benefit for each.

Project

- Students list and analyze places in the community where aerobic endurance activities can take place.

Extending the Lesson

Have students maintain a log of physical activities (include recreation, chores at home, and work) that produce perceived aerobic benefit, such as increased heart and breathing rates and perspiration. For five days students record the names of their activities, the length of their participation, their estimated heart rates, and the estimated calories they used. Then they analyze the amount of time they spent daily participating in aerobic activities.

16 Name the Activity Game

High School Level

Type refers to the selection of and participation in an appropriate activity for gaining aerobic endurance benefits. The type of activity you choose depends on your personal goals and aerobic fitness levels.

Purpose

Students will be able to identify the type of activities that will improve and maintain aerobic endurance benefits for the personal goals they choose. They will also be able to identify the difference between aerobic and anaerobic activities.

Equipment Needed

- 8 to 10 outdoor activity stations based on popular sports and activities
- Direction cards for each station
- Paper and pencil or pen for each student

Relationship to National Standards

Physical Education Standard 4: Student achieves and maintains a health-enhancing level of physical fitness—Student demonstrates the skill, knowledge, and desire to monitor and adjust activity levels to meet personal fitness needs.

Health Education Standard 3: Student demonstrates the ability to practice health-enhancing behaviors and reduce health risks—Student demonstrates strategies to improve or maintain personal and family health.

Set Induction

Review the difference between aerobic and anaerobic activities. Ask students to give examples of activities that fit each category, that fit both categories, and that fit neither category.

Procedure

1. Set up a circuit of 8 to 10 stations based on some popular activities or sports, such as hiking, ultimate Frisbee, soccer, baseball, and so on. At each station, a card directs the student to perform all or part of a skill associated with the activity. For example, a soccer station might direct the student to dribble a soccer ball back and forth through a five-yard maze of cones.

2. Have the students rotate through the stations, spending 2 minutes at each station with a 45-second break while traveling between stations.

3. During the travel break, students should determine whether both the skill and the overall activity at the station they have just left was aerobic, anaerobic, both, or neither. They should record their opinions on paper.

Activity	Type
Hiking	*aerobic*

Teaching Hints

Explain to the students the differences between aerobic and anaerobic activities. If they are out of breath and must stop the activity, it is probably anaerobic. Another way of letting students know an activity is aerobic or anaerobic is to explain that the same activity may be aerobic for one person and anaerobic for another.

Closure and Assessment

Written and Oral

• Have the students identify which activities have both aerobic and anaerobic aspects.

Project

• After calculating the training heart rate, have students participate in a variety of activities of their choice. They should record the exercise performed, their exercise heart rates, and which activities were aerobic and anaerobic based on their own training heart rates.

Extending the Lesson

Repeat this activity after the students have had six weeks to improve their aerobic endurance. Have the students identify which, if any, of the activities changed from anaerobic to aerobic for them.

17 | Moving Beyond

High School Level

Improving aerobic endurance requires doing more than usual. The concepts of frequency, intensity, time, and type or specificity (FITT) offer knowledge to choose strategies for doing more, which leads to demonstrating **progression**.

Purpose

Students will learn to build increasing challenges into their personal fitness plans to gain overload benefits. They will demonstrate progression from baseline fitness performance toward a personalized goal, with feedback as needed or requested from the teacher.

Equipment Needed

- PACER tape
- Measured area of 20 meters (21 yards, 32 inches) or a running area equal to 1 mile

Relationship to National Standards

Physical Education Standard 4: Student achieves and maintains a health-enhancing level of physical fitness—Student meets the health-related standards as defined by *FITNESSGRAM*.

Health Education Standard 3: Student demonstrates the ability to practice health-enhancing behaviors and reduce health risks—Student demonstrates strategies to improve or maintain personal and family health.

Set Induction

Review the definition of aerobic endurance. Remind students that an effective health-related fitness program improves fitness, and that these improvements will require a progression. Explain that progression results from increasing time, increasing intensity, or both, within the same type of activity.

Procedure

1. Select an assessment strategy to establish students' baseline aerobic endurance. Choices from the *FITNESSGRAM* include PACER and a one-mile run or walk.
2. Students perform the assessments.
3. Review the goal-setting process, which requires students to set their goals (identify an improved target score) and to select strategies to reach their goals, keeping in mind the FITT principles. Students set their goals and write down their personalized plans (see sample forms in the appendix).
4. Students follow their personalized plans. This includes recording heart rates, time of activity, and total aerobic activity time.
5. Reassess and confidentially report progress to students, using the following:
   - Present a formal, individualized *FITNESSGRAM* report.
   - Provide a chart of standards for students to examine on their own.

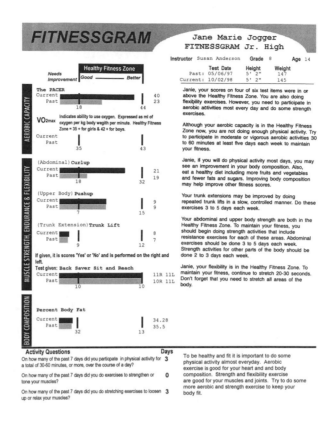

Teaching Hints

Depending on student self-perceptions, there will be a wide range of personal goals and strategies. Some students may want to condition for a sport, and others may wish to reach minimal standards. Some students' goals will not focus on aerobic endurance (for example, a cross-country runner may want to concentrate on muscular strength, because he already has excellent aerobic endurance). Encourage these students to acknowledge progression in their goal setting by planning activities to improve aerobic endurance. You can observe students' daily recordings of heart rate and duration of participation to assist the students in appropriately adjusting the intensity and time to overload workout, using progressive increments.

Closure and Assessment

Written and Oral

* Students review their *FITNESSGRAM* reports and personalized plans. You should ensure that each plan includes warm-up and cool-down activities for major workouts.

Project

* Students prepare assessment records independently, using the standards chart.

Extending the Lesson

* Students create a calendar, graph, or write a journal to record their progress toward their goals.

* Students prepare a personal goal for aerobic endurance improvement. They show how they can incorporate the progression principle into a personal fitness program to improve aerobic endurance.

18 Progressive Endurances

High School Level

Overload requires doing more than usual. Overload for aerobic endurance requires at least one of the following: increasing heart rate within the training zone, exercising for a longer period of time, or exercising more frequently. The concepts of **frequency, intensity, time**, and **type or specificity** (FITT) offer knowledge to choose strategies for doing more, which leads to demonstrating **progression**.

Purpose

Students understand how to develop a long-term plan to improve aerobic fitness.

Equipment Needed

- Workout plans (see appendix)
- Stopwatch or a large clock visible to all

Relationship to National Standards

Physical Education Standard 4: Student achieves and maintains a health-enhancing level of physical fitness—Student demonstrates the skill, knowledge, and desire to monitor and adjust activity levels to meet personal fitness needs.

Health Education Standard 3: Student demonstrates the ability to practice health-enhancing behaviors and reduce health risks—Student demonstrates strategies to improve or maintain personal and family health.

Set Induction

Explain to students that aerobic fitness is a long-term process, not a thing to get ready for a single test. Remind students of the FITT principles, overload, and progression.

Procedure

1. Have each student assess his or her level of aerobic fitness. If a student has not recently completed a *FITNESSGRAM* assessment, have him or her self-assess aerobic fitness using one of the aerobic endurance choices from *FITNESSGRAM*.

2. Introduce the workout plan (appendix) to the students. Remind students that warm-up and cool-down are essential parts of any good workout plan.

3. Have each student prepare a workout plan to improve his or her aerobic fitness. This process should include:
   - Stating clearly the current level of aerobic fitness
   - Setting a challenging, but attainable, goal for improved aerobic fitness
   - Developing a realistic plan for meeting that goal

Fitness Workout Plan

Name: _____   Date: _____

Week Beginning:

Component	Activity	Mon	Tue	Wed	Thu	Fri	Weekend
	Warm-up						
Aerobic Fitness							
Muscular Strength & Endurance							
Flexibility							
Body Composition							
	Cool-down						

Teaching Hints

Encourage students to periodically review their plans so they can identify areas of progress and of need. Depending on student self-perceptions, there will be a wide range of personal goals and strategies. Some students may want to condition for a sport, and others may wish to reach minimal standards. For some who are within the healthy standards at baseline, maintenance may be an appropriate goal for this health-related fitness component.

Closure and Assessment

Written and Oral

- Have students explain the health benefits of reaching the goals specified in their plans.

Project

- Using their FITNESSGRAM test results, along with the information and knowledge students have acquired from the report, have students develop a workout plan incorporating all four aspects of health-related fitness.

Extending the Lesson

Students keep an aerobic activity log book. They set a goal for how much running they would like to be doing at the end of six weeks and note major progressions along the way. They should review and adjust their workout plans after determining how successful they were in both following their workout plans and meeting their fitness goals.

Chapter 9

Muscular Strength and Endurance

1 Warm-Up and Cool-Down

Middle School Level

A **warm-up** is the beginning phase of the training session which helps you prepare your body for activity. Proper warm-up improves the muscles' ability to perform work and helps prevent injuries by increasing blood flow and loosening and stretching muscle fibers and connective tissues (tendons and ligaments). **Cool-down** is gradually tapering back to a resting phase after completing the muscular strength and endurance phase of training. Proper cool-down reduces muscle soreness and allows muscles to flush wastes generated by exercise.

Purpose

Students will understand the importance of a thorough warm-up and cool-down for proper exercise.

Equipment Needed

- Mats

Relationship to National Standards

Physical Education Standard 4: Student achieves and maintains a health-enhancing level of physical fitness—Student demonstrates the skill, knowledge, and desire to monitor and adjust activity levels to meet personal fitness needs.

Health Education Standard 3: Student will demonstrate the ability to practice health-enhancing behaviors and reduce health risks—Student will demonstrate strategies to improve or maintain personal health.

Set Induction

Define the purposes of warm-up and cool-down and their relationship to today's activities. Emphasize that daily activity needs a proper warm-up and cool-down.

Procedure

1. Divide the class into groups of four. Have two people in the group design a warm-up activity and the other two design a cool-down activity for a specific weight-training circuit.

2. Once they have designed the warm-up, the students teach it to the others in the group.

3. All students do the weight-training circuit; then the other students teach the cool-down to the group.

4. Each student evaluates the effects of the warm-up and cool-down on their bodies and their performances.

Teaching Hints

The warm-up and cool-down should each include 5 to 10 minutes of aerobic activity, with stretching of the major muscle groups.

Closure and Assessment

Written and Oral

- Have the students describe how their bodies respond to the warm-up and cool-down, and how the warm-up and cool-down relate to their performance of the weight-training circuit.

Extending the Lesson

Have the students collect photographs or images of individuals performing proper warm-up and cool-down activities.

2 Circuit Training

Middle School Level

Muscular strength is a maximal exertion of the muscle's ability to generate force against resistance for one repetition. **Muscular endurance** is the ability of the muscle to generate force against resistance several to many times. **Strength training** is the process of exercising the muscles with appropriately progressive workloads to strengthen the body.

Purpose

Students will be able to continuously participate in a variety of motivational strength-enhancing activities, challenges, and exercises. Students will understand the difference between muscle endurance and muscle strength and the need to have a balanced strength and endurance program. Students will understand the importance of training each muscle group (see appendix for muscle chart).

Equipment Needed

- Station cards
    1. Isometric—tennis ball squeeze
    2. Plyometric—spot jumping
    3. Weight and resistance training—partner resistance
    4. Calisthenics—curl-up ball pass to partner
    5. Isotonic—biceps curls
- Equipment depending on the exercises

Relationship to National Standards

Physical Education Standard 4: Student achieves and maintains a health-enhancing level of physical fitness—Student correctly demonstrates activities to improve and maintain muscular strength and endurance.

Health Education Standard 3: Student will demonstrate the ability to practice health-enhancing behaviors and reduce health risks—Student will demonstrate strategies to improve or maintain personal health.

Set Induction

Introduce the concepts of muscular strength and muscular endurance. Discuss several examples of muscular strength (high-resistance weight lifting, short sprinting, jumping, throwing) and muscular endurance (low-resistance weight lifting, swimming, jump-roping, tug-of-war). Ask the students to distinguish between the strength and endurance activities.

Procedure

1. Design a 9- to 12-station circuit that develops muscular strength and endurance. These activities may include traditional strength challenges, such as *FITNESSGRAM* curl-ups and push-ups, or partner challenges, such as push-ups hand touch, partner curl-ups with ball pass, spot jumping, and so on.

2. At each station, include a strength information item, such as definitions of muscular strength and endurance and information on proper form. Students should be ready to discuss the information after completing the circuit.

3. Students should work at their individual levels of ability at each station for 20 to 40 seconds. They should take a rest period of 30 seconds while reading the material after moving to the next station.

4. Designate one station as Muscle Motivators. Muscle Motivators move around the room and coach students to use proper form while doing exercises and working toward their personal best!

5. Use a prerecorded tape or 20 to 40 seconds of exercise followed by a 30-second rest. Students perform the strength activity on the first phase, then jog to the next station and stretch the muscle group while reading the new information until the music starts.

Teaching Hints

Use drawings and pictures, along with a list of critical elements, to ensure quality exercises. Include information about the muscle groups for each activity. You may want to use the rest stage to discuss information. Allow middle schoolers to choose their starting station and work with a partner of the same ability level.

Emphasize safety rules with strength training: correct form and posture; awareness of capability levels; slow, smooth movement; and breathing upon exertion.

Closure and Assessment

Written and Oral

• Have students explain their feelings about the two types of muscular activity. How does the muscle feel? How were they breathing during the different activities?

• Have the students explain how improving muscular strength (or endurance) will improve their performance or satisfaction with their favorite sport or physical activity.

Project

• Have students go around the classroom and identify their classmates' favorite strength-training activity. How many students prefer muscular strength activities? Muscular endurance activities?

Extending the Lesson

• Define muscle strength and endurance. Have students develop a list of physical activities that will develop muscular strength and endurance.

• Have students list activities in daily life that require muscular strength and endurance.

• Muscle a day—select a muscle group each day and have students identify muscular strength and endurance activities associated with the muscle.

• Have students explain how muscular strength and endurance can prevent injury in sport, at home, or at school.

3 Go for the Team Gold

Middle School Level

Muscular strength and **muscular endurance** are important in the musculoskeletal function of the body. They contribute to ideal body composition, improve bone density, improve posture, prevent injuries, and help perform tasks of daily living and work.

Purpose

Students will describe the benefits and correctly perform the strength and endurance exercises.

Equipment Needed

- Prepared task cards with various exercises
- Proper equipment for performing the activities on the task cards, such as mats, curl-up strips, and so on
- Paper and pencils for recording progress
- Corbin and Lindsey's *Fitness For Life* muscular-strength activities with exercises and benefits listed

Relationship to National Standards

Physical Education Standard 4: Student achieves and maintains a health-enhancing level of physical fitness—Student correctly demonstrates activities designed to improve and maintain muscular strength and endurance.

Health Education Standard 3: Student will demonstrate the ability to practice health-enhancing behaviors and reduce health risks—Student will demonstrate strategies to improve or maintain personal health.

Set Induction

Review the role of strength training in not only providing strong muscles, but how strength training can assist in correct posture, reduce low back pain, and promote healthy circulatory systems and body composition.

Procedure

1. Design task cards with strength exercises written on one side. Include exercises that help strengthen the back and correct posture, such as reverse curl, trunk lift, arm and leg lift, one-quarter curl-ups, and lower-body lift, as well as other exercises. You may include pictures of the exercises.

2. Have groups of three students choose one strength task. Give each group two to three minutes to discuss their exercise. Each

REVERSE
CURL

group will describe the exercise they chose, explain the health benefits of the exercise, and lead the group in a 30-second set of the exercise. Assign each member a responsibility or role such as the following:

- Strength trainer describes the exercise to the class.
- Medical expert explains the exercise benefits.
- Olympic athlete uses correct form and performs the exercise during the discussion.

3. The group then leads the entire class in a 30-second set of the exercises. Groups take turns leading the exercises, allowing students to complete as many repetitions as they can during 30 seconds, not to exceed 15 repetitions.

Teaching Hints

Review the safety tips for strength-training exercises: proper form, muscular balance, and exhaling upon exertion. The second time you teach this lesson, complete a continuous exercise routine, with students taking turns leading the exercise they led the previous meeting.

Closure and Assessment

Written and Oral

- Have students explain how the benefits obtained from strength training extend beyond muscle development.
- Have each student identify at least one health-related benefit from engaging in regular strength-training activity.

Project

- Have students gather three pictures each associated with the benefits of strength training as it assists health-related fitness.

Extending the Lesson

- Have students list and describe how to use muscle strength and endurance at home and in their daily lives.
- Ask students to identify health problems related to muscular weakness and health risks associated with aging. They can interview a senior citizen who is physically active to determine what strengthening exercises he or she has done. Some students may want to go to a local fitness club and ask participants about their motivation in lifting weights.
- Suggest that students visit a rehabilitation clinic where patients are being treated for musculoskeletal disorders. Ask them to describe the strength-training program that patients are doing. Have students answer the following questions: What caused the problem? How is strength training helping the patients?
- Instruct students to design a strength-training program for developing strong abdominals and backs.

4 Fitness Choices

Middle School Level

Frequency is how often an activity is performed. For strength training, this refers to how often specific muscle groups should be worked and rested during a given time period.

Purpose

Students will identify exercises they can perform every other day. They will identify the muscles they use in everyday activity.

Equipment Needed

- Weights or other appropriate resistance equipment
- Journal report cards
- Chutes and Ladders game board (if doing that activity)

Relationship to National Standards

Physical Education Standard 3: Student exhibits a physically active lifestyle—Student participates regularly in health-enhancing physical activities to accomplish these goals (in and out of the physical education class).

Health Education Standard 3: Student will demonstrate the ability to practice health-enhancing behaviors and reduce health risks—Student will demonstrate strategies to improve or maintain personal health.

Set Induction

Define frequency as it relates to strength-training activities. Explain that each person is unique in how frequently he or she should engage in resistance activities. Discuss the importance of resting muscle groups between strength- and endurance-training sessions.

Procedure

1. Provide a variety of muscular strength choice activities such as the following:
   - Parachute fitness—biceps curls, rowing, deltoid lift, triceps extension, lateral deltoid raise, curl-ups, trunk lift
   - Chutes and Ladders game— add strength activities for each space on the game board
   - Exercise task card—see p. 126
2. Students choose an activity and log it in their journals to get a start keeping a journal.

Day	Activity
Monday	*curl-ups*
Tuesday	
Wednesday	*trunk lift*
Thursday	
Friday	
Saturday	
Sunday	

Teaching Hints

Establish the parameters for each student's journal. The activities may or may not be the same. The teacher may provide a list of potential activities for in and out of school. Develop a class log in which students can report their class members' activities as a way of motivating students to complete this task.

Closure and Assessment

Written and Oral

- Have each student state his or her understanding of frequency.

Project

- Share with classmates activities that show or define frequency in strength training.

Extending the Lesson

- Students develop a fun and fitness choice routine such as the following:
    - Macarena push-ups
    - Alphabet push-ups
    - Chin juggling push-ups
    - Push-up position hockey
- In class, construct a FITT bulletin board, emphasizing that F = frequency. Students can provide daily activities and strength activities that use muscular strength and endurance.

5 Intensity Circuit

Middle School Level

Intensity refers to the level of resistance or interval. You establish intensity levels to permit multiple repetitions. Using heavier weights and fewer repetitions improves strength. Using lighter weights and more repetitions improves endurance. The purpose of the individual's fitness program may affect intensity levels.

Purpose

Students will be able to perform a circuit-training program of strength activities at their personal ability levels.

Equipment Needed

- Wall charts with the progression for each exercise, from easiest to most difficult, including information on fitness target zones for muscular strength and endurance so students can set personal fitness goals
- Weight or resistance equipment

Relationship to National Standards

Physical Education Standard 4: Student achieves and maintains a health-enhancing level of physical fitness—Student understands and applies training principles to improve physical fitness.

Health Education Standard 3: Student will demonstrate the ability to practice health-enhancing behaviors and reduce health risks—Student will demonstrate strategies to improve or maintain personal health.

Set Induction

Define *circuit training* in the context of strength training. Review the differences between circuit training and standard weight lifting. Explain that circuit training involves work-to-rest ratio periods.

Procedure

1. Set up stations for major muscle groups, including upper body, abdominals, arms, shoulders, and legs. At each station, provide at least three options for performing the exercise, modified by the amount of weight students will lift.
2. Students try all options and record the results, up to 15 repetitions for each exercise.
3. Set a goal for improvement, establishing realistic intensity levels for each muscle group. Record the number of repetitions that students can perform with good form, not to exceed 15 repetitions as a starting point.
4. Students should perform two sets of 15 repetitions three times a week until they meet their goals or for at least four weeks. If students can perform more than 15 repetitions, they should add weight or resistance.

Teaching Hints

Encourage proper form at all intensities. You can list exercises by level of difficulty, using skier's signs as follows: green circle for beginner, blue rectangle for recreational, black diamond for expert, and double black diamond for extreme sport professional. Students can make intensity increases by using weights or changing the exercises (e.g., sit-ups, wall push-ups, flat push-ups, and push-ups increase intensity when you elevate the feet). Students must maintain proper form in all options.

The standard work-to-rest ratio for circuit strength training activities is one unit of work to three units of rest.

Closure and Assessment

Written and Oral

- Ask the students to distinguish the work-to-rest ratio for strength training from the work-to-rest ratio for aerobic activity. Why is there more "work" than "rest" in aerobic activity, but more "rest" than "work" in strength training?

- Have students identify the degree of difficulty of today's circuit-training activities, and rate the intensity (light, moderate, or heavy).

Project

- Have students devise additional activities that could be included in a circuit-training routine. Encourage students to include activities that do not require special equipment.

Extending the Lesson

- Students describe pictures of occupations that require differing levels of muscle strength and endurance, for example, secretary and accountant—light intensity; medical doctor, gardener, and carpenter—moderate intensity; farmer, athlete, dancer, and highway construction worker—heavy intensity.

- Students interview people in other occupations about the need for muscular strength and endurance in completing their jobs.

- Suggest that students keep a journal of how they feel when doing strength-training activities.

- Describe what happens when a muscle is not used.

6 Sets and Repetitions

Middle School Level

Time refers to the length of exercise or activity. Time is determined by the number of sets, repetitions, and muscle groups in the workout. To improve strength, work out at high intensity with few repetitions. To improve endurance, work out at low intensity and increase repetitions.

Purpose

The students will be able to determine the pattern of exercise they need to improve muscular strength and the pattern they need to improve endurance by performing resistance exercises.

Equipment Needed

- Mats

Relationship to National Standards

Physical Education Standard 4: Student achieves and maintains a health-enhancing level of physical fitness—Student understands and applies training principles to improve physical fitness.

Health Education Standard 3: Student will demonstrate the ability to practice health-enhancing behaviors and reduce health risks—Student will demonstrate strategies to improve or maintain personal health.

Set Induction

Review the differences between muscular strength and muscular endurance. Discuss the importance of performing activities that require both muscular strength and muscular endurance.

Procedure

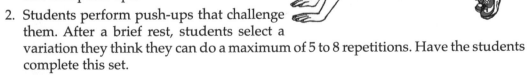

1. Students choose a variation of a push-up that they can perform 15 times with correct form. The variations could include wall push-ups, modified push-ups, regular push-ups, inverted push-ups, and one-arm push-ups.
2. Students perform push-ups that challenge them. After a brief rest, students select a variation they think they can do a maximum of 5 to 8 repetitions. Have the students complete this set.
3. Discuss how intensity modifies time and the number of repetitions in developing muscular strength and endurance. Repeat with other exercises.

Teaching Hints

Students may use resistance bands, bicycle inner tubes, hand weights or leg weights, or surgical tubing to perform this activity with exercises such as biceps curl, leg press, chest press, and so on. Change the intensity of the exercises by adjusting the weight or shortening and lengthening the bands, which will change the strength and endurance demands of the exercise.

Closure and Assessment

Written and Oral

- Have students list, on paper, activities that support muscular strength and muscular endurance, then describe which activities are better for each aspect.
- Have students assign sets and repetitions to each activity, then place these workouts in columns for muscular strength and muscular endurance.

Project

- Have the students track their workouts for one week using the workouts they created for the written assessment.

Extending the Lesson

- Compare different ways to measure the duration that students need to develop each factor of fitness: aerobics = distance and time; strength = weight and repetitions.
- Students make a resistance-training safety poster with guidelines for teenagers: Avoid unsafe weightloads; Use proper form; Exhale on exertion.

7 Muscle-Maker Menus

Middle School Level

This material defines the **type** of activity as it relates to training specificity. Exercises or activities must be specific to the muscle groups and the desired strength or endurance outcome.

Purpose

Students will demonstrate the activities or exercises they need for specific muscle groups to develop muscular strength and endurance.

Equipment Needed

- Depends on student choices
- Music (encourage students to use music during their presentations)
- Pencils
- Poster board
- Butcher paper

Relationship to National Standards

Physical Education Standard 4: Student achieves and maintains a health-enhancing level of physical fitness—Student understands and applies training principles to improve physical fitness.

Health Education Standard 3: Student will demonstrate the ability to practice health-enhancing behaviors and reduce health risks—Student will demonstrate strategies to improve or maintain personal health.

Set Induction

Review the specificity of training a particular muscle group for muscular strength and for muscular endurance. Discuss the importance of training activities that incorporate multiple muscle groups, as opposed to training a single muscle group.

Procedure

1. Students select a muscle group they would like to develop. Form a group of two to four students that have the same muscle group.
2. Students develop a muscle-maker menu for the specific muscle. Give each group a blank muscle-maker menu on which they complete the following: (1) the name and a drawing of the muscle group, (2) the action of the muscle group, (3) the location of the muscle group, (4) specific exercises and activities to target this muscle group, and (5) ways to vary the intensity of the exercise.
3. Divide the tasks up within the group. Students will present their menus to the class and lead them in muscle-maker exercises. Each student will be responsible to lead one activity for the class.

Teaching Hints

Have resources available for student use. Encourage students to use music during their presentations. Allow older students to use resistance equipment.

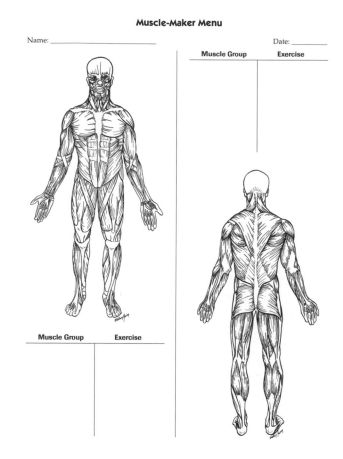

Muscle-Maker Menu

Name: _____   Date: _____

Muscle Group   Exercise

Muscle Group   Exercise

Closure and Assessment

Written and Oral

- Have the student identify which body part they trained by pointing or describing. Have students identify which body part they will train next.

Project

- Make a project score sheet checklist. Students give peer feedback to others by using the checklist.

Extending the Lesson

- Strength bank—Each student develops a strength card to contribute to the strength bank or collection of strength activities. Students may use fitness magazines, sport books, and so on for resources. They should include the name of the activity or exercise, its critical elements, the muscles it improves, and a picture of the activity. Keep the cards filed by muscle groups and available for students to choose from during subsequent days.
- Students prepare a weight-training program for themselves based on their favorite activities.
- Students prepare a weight-training program for one of their family members.
- Students design a poster titled: Why Strength Train?
- Students play strength tic-tac-toe by designing a tic-tac-toe board listing nine different muscle groups. They choose a strength exercise that exercises this muscle group, such as abdominals—curl-ups, quadriceps—wall squats, and arms—biceps curls. They can perform their tic-tac-toe game with family or friends.

8   Making Progress

Middle School Level

The goal of improving muscular strength and endurance (demonstrating progress) requires doing more than usual with your muscles. The concepts of **frequency, intensity, time**, and **type or specificity** (FITT) offer knowledge to choose strategies for doing more, which leads to demonstrating **progression**.

Purpose

Students will demonstrate progression from baseline toward a realistic goal, which they select, with support as needed from the teacher.

Equipment Needed

- Equipment required for the assessment items the teacher chooses
- Record sheets for the assessment
- Goal-setting worksheets
- Curl-up strips and cadence tape for curl-ups
- Cadence tape for push-ups
- Modified pull-up bar for modified pull-ups
- Pull-up bar for pull-ups and flexed-arm hang

Relationship to National Standards

Physical Education Standard 4: Student achieves and maintains a health-enhancing level of fitness—Student meets the health-related standard as defined by *FITNESSGRAM*.

Health Education Standard 3: Student will demonstrate the ability to practice health-enhancing behaviors and reduce health risks—Student will demonstrate strategies to improve or maintain personal health.

Set Induction

Review the four FITT principles (Frequency, Intensity, Time, and Type). Ask the students whether continuing to perform the identical workout over a long period of time will lead to continued improvements in fitness.

Procedure

1. Select an assessment strategy to establish students' baseline for muscular strength and endurance. Choices from the *FITNESSGRAM* include curl-ups, push-ups, modified push-ups, pull-ups, flexed-arm hang, and trunk lift.

2. Students perform the selected assessments.

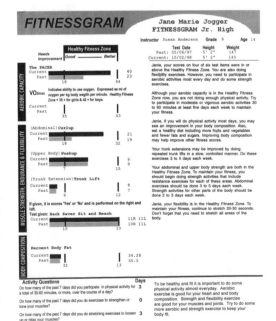

3. Discuss the goal-setting process.
   - Students set their goals (for example, identify an improved score).
   - Students choose their strategies (teacher can supply strategies or students can brainstorm).
   - Students record their plans (see sample forms in appendix).
4. Students follow their plans.
5. Reassess and look for progress in students' performance. Remind them to respect the efforts of others and to keep scores confidential. You might use:
   - A formal, individualized *FITNESSGRAM* report
   - A chart of standards for students to examine on their own

Teaching Hints

Refer to the *FITNESSGRAM* materials to find the standards for the healthy fitness zone for each assessment.

Closure and Assessment

Written and Oral

- Have the students write a short definition of each FITT principle. Discuss the definitions as a group.

Project

- Have the students track their progress over a six-week period.

Extending the Lesson

- Students keep a progress log of personal best challenges.
- Students choose one *FITNESSGRAM* muscular strength and endurance test at the beginning of a six-week period. Over the next six weeks, they should engage in a progressive set of activities to improve their performance on that specific test. They should set a realistic goal and retest at the end of the six weeks. Then they can describe the progression they experienced.

9 Warm-Up and Cool-Down

High School Level

A **warm-up** will increase the temperature of the body and the elasticity of the muscles. A warm-up improves the muscles' ability to perform work and reduces the risk of injury. The **cool-down** is the reverse process of the warm-up. It reduces muscle soreness and brings the body temperature back to normal ranges. Warm-up and cool-down should include some aerobic activity and stretching. The stretching exercises must be specific to the muscle groups you are using during the workout.

Purpose

Students will design a warm-up and cool-down to demonstrate to the class.

Equipment Needed

- Mats

Relationship to National Standards

Physical Education Standard 4: Student achieves and maintains a health-enhancing level of physical fitness—Student demonstrates the skill, knowledge, and desire to monitor and adjust activity levels to meet personal fitness needs.

Health Education Standard 3: Student will demonstrate the ability to practice health-enhancing behaviors and reduce health risks—Student will demonstrate strategies to improve or maintain personal health.

Set Induction

Define the purposes of warm-up and cool-down and their relationship to today's activities. Emphasize that daily activity needs a proper warm-up and cool-down.

Procedure

1. Divide the class into groups of four. Have two people in the group design a warm-up activity and the other two design a cool-down activity for a specific weight-training circuit.
2. Once they have designed the warm-up, the students teach it to the others in the group.
3. All students do the weight-training circuit; then the other students teach the cool-down to the group.
4. Each student evaluates the effects of the warm-up and cool-down on their bodies and their performances.

Teaching Hints

The warm-up and cool-down should each include 5 to 10 minutes of aerobic activity, with stretching of the major muscle groups. Add balls, towels, hoops, and other items to give variety in activities.

Closure and Assessment

Written and Oral

- Have the students describe how their bodies respond to the warm-up and cool-down, and how the warm-up and cool-down relate to their performance of the weight-training circuit.

Extending the Lesson

Have the students collect photographs or images of individuals performing proper warm-up and cool-down activities.

10 | Moving Beyond

High School Level

The goal of improving muscular strength and endurance (demonstrating progress) requires doing more than usual with your muscles. The concepts of **frequency, intensity, time**, and **type or specificity** (FITT) offer knowledge to choose strategies for doing more, which leads to demonstrating **progression**.

Purpose

Students will demonstrate progression from baseline toward a realistic goal, which they select, with support as needed from the teacher.

Equipment Needed

- Equipment required for the assessment items the teacher chooses
- Record sheets for the assessment
- Goal-setting worksheets
- Pull-up bar for pull-ups
- Curl-up strips and cadence tape for curl-ups
- Modified pull-up bar for modified pull-ups
- Cadence tape for push-ups
- Pull-up bar for flexed-arm hang

Relationship to National Standards

Physical Education Standard 4: Student achieves and maintains a health-enhancing level of fitness—Student meets the health-related standard as defined by *FITNESSGRAM*.

Health Education Standard 3: Student will demonstrate the ability to practice health-enhancing behaviors and reduce health risks—Student will demonstrate strategies to improve or maintain personal health.

Set Induction

Define the four principles of FITT (Frequency, Intensity, Time, and Type). Offer several examples, and ask the students to share their examples. Demonstrate the activities you've chosen to use from the first step of the procedure below.

Procedure

1. Select an assessment strategy to establish students' baseline for muscular strength and endurance. Choices from the *FITNESSGRAM* include curl-ups, push-ups, modified push-ups, pull-ups, flexed-arm hang, and trunk lift.

2. Students perform the selected assessments.

3. Review the goal-setting process, which requires students to set their goals (i.e., identify an im-

proved score) and to select strategies to reach their goals, keeping in mind the FITT principles. Students set their goals and write down their personalized plans (see sample forms in appendix).

4. Students follow their personalized plans.

5. Reassess and look for progress in students' performance. Remind students to respect the efforts of others and to keep scores confidential. You might use a formal, individualized *FITNESSGRAM* report or a chart of standards for students to examine on their own.

Teaching Hints

Depending on student self-perceptions, there will be a wide range of personal goals and strategies. Some students may want to condition for a sport, and others may wish to reach minimal standards. For some who are within the healthy standards at baseline, maintenance may be a goal instead of demonstrating progression.

Closure and Assessment

Written and Oral

- Students report that on reassessment they improve or maintain their muscular strength and endurance.

Extending the Lesson

- Students describe how to modify a weight-training program with the rules of overload and progression for the following situations:
  - Patient with high blood pressure
  - Cardiac patient
  - Adult working on muscular tone
  - Athlete involved in a contact sport
  - Athlete interested in endurance and lifetime sport
  - Grandparent
  - Elementary school child
  - Someone who wants to increase muscle tone
- Students develop a three-month strength-training program demonstrating progression and overload.
- Students interview an athletic trainer who works with a sport. They can ask about the field and techniques in developing a strength-training program.

11 Personal Best Challenges

High School Level

Progression is a sequential change in frequency, intensity, and/or time. **Overload** is an increase in frequency, intensity, or time beyond the body's normal capacity. Levels of overload should be based upon an individual's fitness goals.

Purpose

Students will define the overload and progression principles of exercise.

Equipment Needed

- Personal best challenge activity cards
- Personal best record sheets
- Stopwatch
- Pencils

Relationship to National Standards

Physical Education Standard 4: Student achieves and maintains a health-enhancing level of physical fitness—Student understands and applies training principles to improve physical fitness.

Health Education Standard 3: Student will demonstrate the ability to practice health-enhancing behaviors and reduce health risks—Student will demonstrate strategies to improve or maintain personal health.

Set Induction

Discuss frequency, intensity, and time as they relate to progression and overload. Ensure the students understand the significant differences between progression and overload.

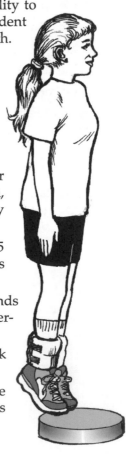

Procedure

1. Develop a personal best challenge menu of activities for your students to choose from (push-ups, chair dips, push-up fun, curl-ups, etc.) for this activity. Each student chooses the activity he or she would like to participate in to improve fitness.

2. On day one, students participate in their selected activity for 15 seconds and repeat it a second time. Students record their scores on a personal best record sheet.

3. On day two, they repeat the activity for two rounds of 15 seconds again. The class can discuss overload and progression and determine which occurred.

4. On day three, increase the time requirement to 20 seconds. Ask students if overload or progression occurred and why.

5. Continue for the remainder of the week, increasing the time segment to 25 seconds. Students continue to record their scores and reach a personal best by week's end.

Teaching Hints

Practice each activity with the students before they select their activity. Remind them that their goal is to improve their own performance, not to compare their performance with others.

Closure and Assessment

Written and Oral

- Ask students to define overload and progression, give examples of activities, and illustrate overload and progression in the activities they present.

Project

- Have the students develop a written plan to demonstrate overload using a personal challenge activity without varying the time. Students should develop plans for varying frequency and for varying intensity.

Extending the Lesson

Explain and discuss the training principles in overload and progression, and apply them to muscular strength and endurance. In class, design a chart illustrating overload and progression in a strength exercise and an endurance exercise.

12 Circuit Training

High School Level

Muscular strength is a maximal exertion of the muscle's ability to generate force against resistance for one repetition. **Muscular endurance** is the ability of the muscle to generate force against resistance several to many times. **Strength training** is the process of exercising the muscles with appropriately progressive workloads to strengthen the body.

Purpose

Students will participate in a circuit-training course that allows them to experience the differences in muscular strength and endurance exercises, and identify the four types of strength-training equipment. In addition, they will be able to develop a strength-training program based on their personal needs.

Equipment Needed

- Dumbbells of various weights
- Resistance bands
- Steps
- Weight machines

Relationship to National Standards

Physical Education Standard 4: Student achieves and maintains a health-enhancing level of physical fitness—Student demonstrates the skill, knowledge, and desire to monitor and adjust activity levels to meet personal fitness needs.

Health Education Standard 3: Student will demonstrate the ability to practice health-enhancing behaviors and reduce health risks—Student will demonstrate strategies to improve or maintain personal health.

Set Induction

Introduce the concepts of muscular strength and muscular endurance. Discuss several examples of muscular strength (high-resistance weight lifting, short sprinting, jumping, throwing) and muscular endurance (low-resistance weight lifting, swimming, jump-roping, tug-of-war). Ask the students to distinguish between the strength and endurance activities.

Procedure

1. Design a circuit that allows the students to work in pairs and become familiar with the major muscle groups, weight-training equipment, correct form for exercise performance, and safety rules.
2. The circuit should involve different ways to adapt strength training for personal needs (weight bearing, free weight, and machines). Suggested circuits are as follows:

Muscle	Body weight	Free resistance (weights & bands)	Machine resistance
Calf	Heel raise	Weighted heel raise	Standing heel raise
Quadriceps	Lunge on a step	Weighted lunge	Leg extension
Hamstrings	Squat	Resistance band curl	Leg curl
Hip adductors	Side leg lift	Leg lift with ankle weight	Hip adductor machine
Hip abductors	Leg lift	Leg lift with ankle weight	Hip abductor machine
Gluteals	Squat	Squat or lunge	Leg press
Low back	Chest lift	Chest lift	Low back machine
Abdominals	Curl-up	Curl-up	Curl machine
Pectorals	Push-up	Dumbbell press	Chest press
Lats	Chin-up	Bent-over row	Lat pull
Deltoids	Inverted push-up	Dumbbell lateral raise	Lateral raise
Biceps	Chin-up	Dumbbell curl	Biceps curl
Triceps	Dips	Triceps extension	Triceps extension

Teaching Hints

Remind students of the following safety rules: maintain control at a moderate pace, keep records, exhale on exertion, maintain stability, emphasize form, follow time specified at each station, follow station arrangement at your own rate (i.e., alternate stations using free weights, weight machines, and body weight). Encourage students to start with a low weight and gradually build up. Have students do 12 to 15 repetitions for endurance and 4 to 8 for strength training.

Closure and Assessment

Written and Oral

- Ask students to identify muscle groups involved with today's activity. Discuss the benefits of circuit training for developing muscular strength and muscular endurance.

Project

- Have students design a strength-training circuit regimen that would fit in a 20-minute block of time. The regimen must include rest periods and time for movement between stations. The students may choose to develop either muscular strength or muscular endurance with this regimen.

Extending the Lesson

Students analyze a sport skill in which strength and endurance are necessary and modify the circuit to enhance the muscle groups they need for this specific skill.

13 Health Benefits of Exercise

High School Level

Muscular strength and **muscular endurance** are important in the proper functioning of the body. They contribute to ideal body composition, improve bone density, improve posture, prevent injuries, and help perform the tasks of daily living and work.

Purpose

The students will understand the benefits of muscular strength and endurance.

Equipment Needed

- Paper and pen or pencil

Relationship to National Standards

Physical Education Standard 4: Student achieves and maintains a health-enhancing level of physical fitness—Student develops a relationship of strength and endurance to specific health conditions.

Health Education Standard 3: Student will demonstrate the ability to practice health-enhancing behaviors and reduce health risks—Student will demonstrate strategies to improve or maintain personal health.

Set Induction

Define muscular strength and muscular endurance. Describe several daily activities that are examples of each.

Procedure

1. Students conduct a case study. Bring an athletic trainer or physical therapist into the class to provide details about an athlete in rehabilitation following injury.
2. Other individuals who may provide good classroom examples include a person in rehabilitation following joint replacement or another serious joint injury, a strength and conditioning specialist, or an athlete engaged in a specific strength and endurance training program.

Teaching Hints

Present background information and resources, defining terms; describing expectations of training and conditioning programs for prevention and rehabilitation; and describing muscular and structural problems such as osteoporosis, muscular dystrophy, joint replacement, degeneration, and so on.

Closure and Assessment

Written and Oral

- Have the students discuss how the information in today's activity concerns their own strength and fitness goals.

Extending the Lesson

Students visit other appropriate agencies and professionals to learn more about strength-training needs in specific contexts. Some examples include:

- Students interview a senior citizen who is physically active to determine what strength activities he or she does.
- Students go to a local fitness club to ask participants about their motivation in lifting weights.
- Students visit emergency personnel to learn their strength and endurance needs while responding to emergencies.

14 Weight-Training Log

High School Level

Frequency is how often you should perform strength training.

Purpose

Students will perform, experience, and log the benefit of various strength and endurance exercises three times a week for an extended period.

Equipment Needed

- Log sheets
- Free weights, weight machines, or body weight
- Diagram of workouts and facility layout

Relationship to National Standards

Physical Education Standard 3: Student exhibits a physically active lifestyle—Student participates regularly in health-enhancing physical activities to accomplish their goals in and out of the physical education class.

Physical Education Standard 4: Student achieves and maintains a health-enhancing level of physical fitness—Student has skills, knowledge, interest, and desire to independently maintain an active lifestyle throughout life.

Health Education Standard 3: Student will demonstrate the ability to practice health-enhancing behaviors and reduce health risks—Student will demonstrate strategies to improve or maintain personal health.

Set Induction

Define frequency and its relationship to a weekly training log. Help students understand the specific muscle groups to be worked, the days of each workout, and the rest period between workouts.

Procedure

1. Students will keep a log of their selected weight-training activities to demonstrate frequency of involvement.
2. They will record the dates they trained, the activities, repetitions, and resistance used. The log should cover two months.

Teaching Hints

Use log sheets supplied in the appendix.

Muscular Strength and Endurance Training Log

Name: _____

Date: _____

Monday		Week 1		Week 2		Week 3		Week 4		Week 5		Week 6	
	2 × 5		2 × 5		2 × 5		2 × 5		2 × 5		2 × 5		
	2 × 5		2 × 5		2 × 5		2 × 5		2 × 5		2 × 5		
	2 × 10		2 × 10		2 × 10		2 × 10		2 × 10		2 × 10		
	2 × 5		2 × 5		2 × 5		2 × 5		2 × 5		2 × 5		
	2 × 10		2 × 10		2 × 10		2 × 10		2 × 10		2 × 10		
	2 × 5		2 × 5		2 × 5		2 × 5		2 × 5		2 × 5		
	2 × 10		2 × 10		2 × 10		2 × 10		2 × 10		2 × 10		
	2 × 10		2 × 10		2 × 10		2 × 10		2 × 10		2 × 10		

Thursday		Week 1		Week 2		Week 3		Week 4		Week 5		Week 6	
	2 × 5		2 × 5		2 × 5		2 × 5		2 × 5		2 × 5		
	2 × 10		2 × 10		2 × 10		2 × 10		2 × 10		2 × 10		
	2 × 5		2 × 5		2 × 5		2 × 5		2 × 5		2 × 5		
	2 × 5		2 × 5		2 × 5		2 × 5		2 × 5		2 × 5		
	2 × 5		2 × 5		2 × 5		2 × 5		2 × 5		2 × 5		
	2 × 10		2 × 10		2 × 10		2 × 10		2 × 10		2 × 10		
	2 × 10		2 × 10		2 × 10		2 × 10		2 × 10		2 × 10		
	2 × 10		2 × 10		2 × 10		2 × 10		2 × 10		2 × 10		

Date	Comments

Closure and Assessment

Written and Oral

- Have students describe a weekly regimen that includes strength training for both muscular strength and muscular endurance, along with appropriate rest periods.

Project

- Instruct students to create a week-long training program that includes strength training for both muscular strength and muscular endurance, along with appropriate rest periods.

Extending the Lesson

Have students follow a six-week training program and test their progress at the end of the period. Encourage students to revise their training program for continued improvement or to develop different muscle groups.

15 Team Teaching

High School Level

Intensity refers to the level of resistance or interval. You establish intensity levels to permit multiple repetitions. Using heavier weights and fewer repetitions improves strength. Using lighter weights and more repetitions improves endurance. The purpose of the individual's fitness program may affect intensity levels.

Purpose

Students will identify and demonstrate ways to vary intensity in strength-training activities.

Equipment Needed

- Resistance equipment such as weights, resistance bands, or machines
- Mats

Relationship to National Standards

Physical Education Standard 4: Student achieves and maintains a health-enhancing level of physical fitness—Student designs a personal fitness program.

Health Education Standard 3: Student will demonstrate the ability to practice health-enhancing behaviors and reduce health risks—Student will demonstrate strategies to improve or maintain personal health.

Set Induction

Review intensity as it relates to resistance and interval. Help the students understand how intensity permits the improvement of muscular strength and muscular endurance.

Procedure

1. From a list of available activities, have students each select three that interest them.

2. Divide the class into groups of four or fewer according to their activity interests. Each group will analyze their activity for what muscular strength and endurance it requires. Have the group discuss the muscles they use in the activity and design a training program that increases in intensity. The program should show at least three levels of intensity.

3. The group will then perform their program, increasing intensity until they reach their goals. Ask students to compare the programs designed by each group, reflecting on goals and activity needs.

Teaching Hints

Reemphasize safety concerns, such as controlled, continuous movement of the weight; exhaling on exertion; and working at an appropriate level. High school students should be working on activities of personal choice to effect life activity habits beyond the class requirement. Working in groups enables students to share knowledge and encourage each other to succeed.

Closure and Assessment

Written and Oral

- Pair students together and have each pair create a list of strength-training activities using intensity to design an appropriate program.

Project

- Write the headings "Muscular Strength" and "Muscular Endurance" on a chalkboard. Have each pair of students bring their strength-training program up and place it under the appropriate heading.

Extending the Lesson

- Students list and describe activities of daily living and work requiring different levels of strength and endurance.
- Students analyze each of several activities to determine the appropriate levels of muscular strength and muscular endurance. These may include both daily living activities and more unusual activities such as providing emergency assistance.

16 Intensity Circuit

High School Level

Time (duration) is the amount of time you spend performing an exercise. This may depend on the number of sets, number of repetitions, muscle groups involved in the workout, and rest time. **Intensity** refers to the level of resistance or interval. You establish intensity levels to permit multiple repetitions. Using heavier weights and fewer repetitions improves strength. Using lighter weights and more repetitions improves endurance. The purpose of the individual's fitness program may affect intensity levels.

Purpose

The student will learn to create a plan for developing muscular strength and endurance using time and intensity as the key elements of the plan.

Equipment Needed

- Resistance equipment such as free weights, resistance machines, and resistance bands
- Mats

Relationship to National Standards

Physical Education Standard 4: Student achieves and maintains a health-enhancing level of physical fitness—Student demonstrates the skill, knowledge, and desire to monitor and adjust activity levels to meet personal fitness needs.

Health Education Standard 3: Student will demonstrate the ability to practice health-enhancing behaviors and reduce health risks—Student will demonstrate strategies to improve or maintain personal health.

Set Induction

Review the definitions of time and intensity, and their relation to developing muscular strength and endurance in a program setting.

Procedure

1. In a weight room, have each student do a different exercise. Students should select a resistance at which they can do 15 repetitions. Have students execute the exercise correctly.

2. After a brief rest, they can select a resistance at which they believe they can do a maximum of 8 repetitions. They should record this resistance and complete this set.

3. Discuss how intensity and repetitions modify time. Then have the students rotate to a new exercise and repeat the process.

Teaching Hints

Reemphasize safety skills. Introduce appropriate spotting technique. Proper and effective warm-up should be an integral part of the strength-training program. Provide a strength-training poster that shows proper lifting techniques for the selected exercises. Emphasize that students following a muscular workout will notice fatigue lasting up to a day. Encourage them to plan for alternating groups of muscles they will work, to best use their workout time and to rest.

Closure and Assessment

Written and Oral

- Describe a strength-training protocol. Have the students identify the appropriate time and intensity elements of that protocol.

Extending the Lesson

- Students compare the element of time used for a muscular endurance workout with time used for an aerobic workout. They can perform 8 strength exercises that will exercise all major body parts for 1 to 2 sets, 15 repetitions each, with a rest period between each set. Students then perform the same sequence twice, one set at a time, without the rest between sets. Compare the times required to perform each workout.

- Students design a personal plan for developing muscular strength and endurance using an activity they are interested in. They should analyze the time they will need to complete the workout and compare the time they have available. They can plan a daily and weekly schedule, including enough time to reach their goals. Have the students follow the plans they develop for six weeks and evaluate their progress.

17 Design for Specificity

High School Level

Specificity of training refers to the physiological adaptations to exercise that are specific to the system you work during the stress of exercise. For example, strength training is the best way to increase strength, but is not optimal for developing cardiovascular fitness. Training programs should be designed for specific goals and objectives.

Purpose

Students will design a strength-training program specific to an activity or sport of personal interest and accessibility.

Equipment Needed

- Activity cards
- Workout worksheets (see appendix)
- Weights and other sources of resistance, such as medicine balls
- Steps
- Machines

Relationship to National Standards

Physical Education Standard 4: Student achieves and maintains a health-enhancing level of physical fitness—Student designs a personal fitness program.

Health Education Standard 3: Student will demonstrate the ability to practice health-enhancing behaviors and reduce health risks—Student will demonstrate strategies to improve or maintain personal health.

Set Induction

Review the definition of specificity. Help students understand how specificity determines program design, and the importance of a written, outcome-based program design.

Procedure

1. Students choose an activity or sport (hiking, biking, soccer, etc.). Have them develop a strength-training program that will enhance their performance or enjoyment of the activity (see appendix). Ensure that each program includes a variety of strength-training activities.

2. The students will work in pairs. One will take the other through half of the designed workout; then they will switch roles.

Teaching Hints

Students should choose their activities based on personal preference and potential for success, supported by analysis of their motor fitness, their sense of competence, and the activity's accessibility. Although students are in pairs, they can work on different activities, acting as peer coaches for each other. Students should analyze their activities to determine which major muscle groups they use and how much muscular strength and endurance they require for successful performance. They should also assess the resistance level for each muscle group, set goals for their personal plans, and work their plans until they achieve their goals.

Closure and Assessment

Written and Oral

- Develop a written program for strength training using the form in the appendix.

Project

- Have each pair examine another pair's workout programs. How are the other pair's programs different from their own?

Extending the Lesson

While attending a sport function, students can select one player and analyze his or her performance throughout the event. Students should note the player's strengths, common errors, and level of energy. They can also analyze the strength and endurance needs of the activity and suggest a program for improving the observed player.

18 Design for Progression

High School Level

The goal of improving muscular strength and endurance (demonstrating progress) requires doing more than usual with your muscles. The concepts of frequency, intensity, time, and type or specificity (FITT) offer knowledge to choose strategies for doing more, which leads to demonstrating **progression**.

Purpose

Students will improve *FITNESSGRAM* scores or their self-set goals for muscular strength and endurance using the overload and progression principles.

Equipment Needed

- *FITNESSGRAM* test
- Strength-training workout logs

Relationship to National Standards

Physical Education Standard 3: Student exhibits a physically active lifestyle—Student participates regularly in health-enhancing physical activities to accomplish their goals in and out of the physical education class.

Physical Education Standard 4: Student achieves and maintains a health-enhancing level of physical fitness—Student has the skills, knowledge, interest, and desire to independently maintain an active lifestyle throughout his or her life. Student designs a personal fitness program.

Health Education Standard 3: Student will demonstrate the ability to practice health-enhancing behaviors and reduce health risks—Student will demonstrate strategies to improve or maintain personal health.

Set Induction

Review the four FITT principles (Frequency, Intensity, Time, and Type). Ask the students whether continuing to perform the identical workout over a long period of time will lead to continued improvements in fitness.

Procedure

1. Have the students design a strength-training program with at least three levels of progression to meet their personal needs, based on the results of their strength assessment or their individual goals.

2. Review for the students the components of a strength-training program: frequency, intensity, time, and type. Have the students use the program outline in

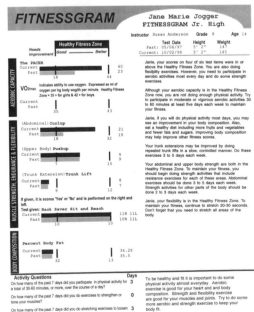

the appendix (or assist them in creating their own format) to design programs in class to best suit their personal needs.

3. After starting their programs, have students record the frequency, intensity, time, and type, how the workout felt, and if they felt improvement.

4. At the end of six weeks, have the students reassess their *FITNESSGRAM* scores in relation to their personal goals. At this time, they will also write an essay explaining the FITT components and how they affected the design of their strength-training programs.

Teaching Hints

Emphasize the factors to consider when designing an exercise program:

- Always make safety a primary concern.
- Train each body segment by working it against a resistance capable of overloading the muscles.
- Perform the exercises through the joints' full range of motion.
- The training speed should be slow and controlled, avoiding swinging, jerking, or momentum.
- Prevent injuries by training those muscle groups that require special attention because of daily misuse, muscular imbalances, or athletic pursuits.
- Provide one day of rest between workouts of the same muscle groups.

Closure and Assessment

Written and Oral

- Discuss how the students' progression and overload are appropriate to the exercise and goals.

Project

- Have the students discuss the relationship of strength training to aerobic endurance, flexibility, and body composition.

Extending the Lesson

Have the students monitor their progress on the program for a period of six weeks. This should include retesting using *FITNESSGRAM* at the end of six weeks.

Chapter 10
Flexibility

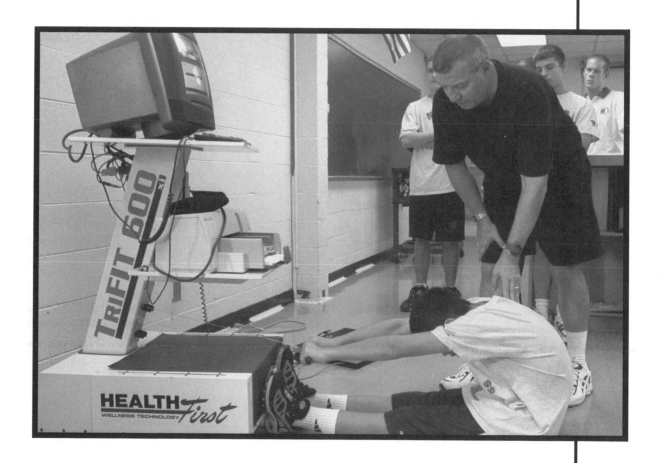

1 Warm-Up for Flexibility

Middle School Level

Warm-up prepares the body for what is to come. Imitating an exercise activity for 5 to 15 minutes before high-intensity workouts improves overall performance. This makes the muscles become aware of the type of movement they will be doing. Students should do stretching after a five-minute aerobic warm-up that allows the muscles to get warm. Stretching in the **cool-down** helps eliminate muscle soreness.

Purpose

Students will be able to create a warm-up routine including both an aerobic heart warm-up and appropriate stretching activities. Students will be able to create a cool-down routine including stretching.

Equipment Needed

- Music tape
- Cones
- Station cards
- Movement cards

Relationship to National Standards

Physical Education Standard 4: Student achieves and maintains a health-enhancing level of physical fitness—Student understands and applies training principles to improve physical fitness.

Health Education Standard 3: Student will demonstrate the ability to practice health-enhancing behaviors and reduce health risks—Student will demonstrate strategies to improve or maintain personal health.

Set Induction

Define warm-up and cool-down. Remind students that muscles and connective tissues stretch more easily and completely when warm than when cold.

Procedure

1. Divide students into groups of 2-4.
2. Have the students warm up for 3-5 minutes.
3. Each group then creates its own 3-5 minute warm-up stretching routine. Routines should
   - Stretch all major muscle groups
   - Stretch both sides of the body
4. After the groups complete the warm-up, remind them to use the same (or similar) stretching routine during cool-down.

Teaching Hints

Make sure the students know the correct form for each stretch. After you have used this activity once or twice, you can have different groups lead the entire class during the stretching portion of the warm-up and cool-down.

Closure and Assessment

Written and Oral

- Ask students to describe how their muscles feel when cold, when warm before stretching, and when warm after stretching.

Project

- Have students write their own stretching programs on index cards to share with the class.

Extending the Lesson

Have students choose a partner. They must each write a stretching program, including all the FITT components, for their partners. They can demonstrate the stretches to their partners and guide them through the program.

2   Flexibility Stations

Middle School Level

Flexibility comes from a joint's ability to move through a full range of motion. There is an optimum range of motion essential for peak performance during activity.

Purpose

The students will identify and demonstrate stretches for various muscle groups.

Equipment Needed

- Cones for flexibility stations
- Paper and pen or pencil for each student
- Mats
- Flexibility cards

Relationship to National Standards

Physical Education Standard 4: Student achieves and maintains a health-enhancing level of physical fitness—Student begins to develop a strategy for improving selected fitness components.

Health Education Standard 3: Student will demonstrate the ability to practice health-enhancing behaviors and reduce health risks—Student will demonstrate strategies to improve or maintain personal health.

Set Induction

Define flexibility. Relate flexibility to preparing for physical activity, including proper warm-up.

Procedure

1. Place flexibility stations around the activity area with flexibility cards. Each card contains the name of the stretch, lists the muscles being stretched, and illustrates the stretch. (There is a sample in the appendix.) Students will form groups of four at the different stations and choose a card.

2. Begin the activity with a power-walk to warm up. The task is for the groups to jog together, locate the flexibility station that exercises the muscle group on the card, and perform the stretch.

3. Students will then jog back to the corner and choose another card.

4. Students write the names of the stretch they used next to the muscle name.

Teaching Hints

Review the location and function of each muscle group students are stretching as well as correct stretching form.

Closure and Assessment

Written and Oral

- Have the students state how one stretch helps the related muscle groups.

Project

- Students discuss the function of the ligaments, tendons, and muscles and how they work together to allow flexion and extension.

Extending the Lesson

Have students design a set of flexibility cards that focuses on preparing for a particular popular sport or activity.

3 | Flexibility Hopscotch

Middle School Level

Keeping your joints flexible with a full range of motion is important in promoting overall health. **Benefits of stretching** include decreased risk of injury in sports, daily chores, and tasks; increased blood supply and nutrients to the joints; reduced muscular soreness after activity; and improved balance, mobility, and posture.

Purpose

Students will recognize and demonstrate correct stretching form and understand the benefits of stretching.

Equipment Needed

- Pictures of stretches (see appendix for samples)
- Benefits of stretching cards
- Beanbags

Relationship to National Standards

Physical Education Standard 3: Student exhibits a physically active lifestyle—Student identifies the critical aspects of a healthy lifestyle.

Health Education Standard 3: Student will demonstrate the ability to practice health-enhancing behaviors and reduce health risks—Student will demonstrate strategies to improve or maintain personal health.

Set Induction

Discuss range of motion, including both what it means and how it applies to preparing oneself for physical activity. Discuss the relationship between joint flexibility and muscle mobility.

Procedure

1. Make a hopscotch board on the floor with nine flexibility activity cards. On each card include a benefit for stretching and a stretch to perform.
2. Divide the class into equal groups and have four groups per game board.
3. Have each group warm up by power-walking or jogging for 2 or 3 minutes.
4. Give each group a beanbag to toss, and have the group members take turns tossing the beanbag and hopping through the hopscotch board. When students toss the beanbag onto the first square, they will go through the hopscotch board. When they return to pick up the beanbag, they will call out the benefit of the next stretch to do.
5. The group will then do the stretch while the next group does the hopscotch board. Remind them to stretch both sides equally.

Teaching Hints

Review the stretches on the cards before class to ensure correct form. Students may draw their own hopscotch game boards outside on the asphalt courts or sidewalks. Provide a flexibility guide and benefit fact sheet to design the hopscotch board.

Closure and Assessment

Written and Oral

- Have students name three benefits of stretching they learned in this lesson.

Project

- Have pairs of students demonstrate a stretch that would effectively assist in improving the flexibility of a joint you specify.

Extending the Lesson

- Students interview an injured athlete. They find out from the trainer what stretching procedures the athlete is doing to regain range of motion.
- Encourage students to teach stretches to other family members.

Flex-a-Day

Middle School Level

Consistent and frequent stretching increases the **range of motion** of a joint, improves circulation, and prepares the muscles to be more effective during physical activity.

Purpose

Students will design a stretching routine to increase flexibility in their daily activities.

Equipment Needed

* Calendar
* Handout including suggested stretches with correct form

Relationship to National Standards

Physical Education Standard 4: Student achieves and maintains a health-enhancing level of physical fitness—Student begins to develop a strategy for improving selected fitness components.

Health Education Standard 3: Student will demonstrate the ability to practice health-enhancing behaviors and reduce health risks—Student will demonstrate strategies to improve or maintain personal health.

Set Induction

Review range of motion and flexibility. State how range of motion and flexibility are involved in preparing for physical activity. Help the students understand the purpose of warming up prior to physical activity.

Procedure

1. Have the students warm up by jogging or power-walking for 2 or 3 minutes.
2. Have students assess flexibility using one or more *FITNESSGRAM* measures.
3. Based on the *FITNESSGRAM* assessment, have each student develop a program to improve flexibility. The plan should include a variety of stretches and should consider all the major muscle groups.
4. Have the students follow their plans for one month. At the end of the month, reassess flexibility using the same *FITNESSGRAM* measure(s) used in step 2 above.

15	16	17	18	19	20	21
hamstring *quads* *hips*		*torso* *quads* *hamstring*			*pecs* *torso* *quads* *neck*	
22	23	24	25	26	27	28

Teaching Hints

Suggest some basic stretches, but encourage students to select stretches that are appropriate for their favorite activities.

Closure and Assessment

Written and Oral

- Pair off students. Have one member of each pair demonstrate a stretch, while the other student states which muscle groups that stretch affects.

Project

- Students choose their favorite stretches and make visual aids showing correct form for that stretch. This might include making a class stretching video showing a variety of stretches.

Extending the Lesson

Students develop a stretching plan for use during short classroom breaks. Emphasize that this stretching plan should not disrupt a classroom environment.

5 Flexibility Circuit

Middle School Level

Time refers to how long to hold a stretch. Students should hold stretches 10 to 15 seconds per suggested stretch, and repeat each stretch (do the stretches two times in a row).

Purpose

Students will understand the importance of holding a stretch for 10 to 15 seconds.

Equipment Needed

- Cones
- Station cards listing two different stretches for each muscle group (chest, shoulders, back, triceps, biceps, quadriceps, hamstrings, calves, abdominals)
- Visible clock with a second hand

Relationship to National Standards

Physical Education Standard 4: Student achieves and maintains a health-enhancing level of physical fitness—Student begins to develop a strategy for improving selected fitness components.

Health Education Standard 3: Student will demonstrate the ability to practice health-enhancing behaviors and reduce health risks—Student will demonstrate strategies to improve or maintain personal health.

Set Induction

Using clay or bubble gum, demonstrate the importance of holding a stretch. First try to bend the clay or gum without working it (it will probably snap). Then work the clay (in your hands) or bubble gum (by chewing) for 10-15 seconds and try to bend it again (it should be much more flexible).

Procedure

1. Place the station cards on the wall in the activity area, allowing enough space near each card for students to perform the listed stretches in groups without crowding.
2. Have the students warm up for 2 or 3 minutes by power-walking, jogging, or using another appropriate activity.
3. Divide the students into as many groups as you have station cards.
4. Send each group to a different station. At the station, the group determines what muscle groups are being stretched and practices each stretch, using the clock to hold the stretch for 10 to 15 seconds. If time permits, students should repeat stretches.
5. After 2 minutes, each group rotates to the next station.

Teaching Hints

Remind students to stretch both sides.

Closure and Assessment

Written and Oral

- Ask students whether it is easier or harder to stretch farther at the end of a 15-second stretch.

Project

- Have students collect pictures showing static stretching for different major muscle groups.

Extending the Lesson

Students visit a training room or rehabilitation clinic and interview a trainer, doctor, or athlete about flexibility practices.

6 Flexion Connection

Middle School Level

Specificity refers to the type of training specific to the system you work during exercise. There are two types of flexibility: static flexibility and dynamic flexibility. Static flexibility is the range of motion around a joint, with little emphasis on speed of movement. Dynamic flexibility refers to the rate of movement at the joint as it relates to improving flexibility. For example, a major league baseball pitcher must have sufficient dynamic flexibility of the shoulder to throw a pitch 90 miles per hour. Both are important for overall fitness, whether related to sports or general activity.

Purpose

Students will demonstrate the types of stretches for different sports and activities.

Equipment Needed

- Muscle charts (see appendix)
- Pencils or pens and clipboards

Relationship to National Standards

Physical Education Standard 3: Student exhibits a physically active lifestyle—Student participates regularly in health-enhancing physical activities to accomplish physical activity goals in and outside the class.

Health Education Standard 3: Student will demonstrate the ability to practice health-enhancing behaviors and reduce health risks—Student will demonstrate strategies to improve or maintain personal health.

Set Induction

Define static flexibility and dynamic flexibility. Remind students that both aspects of flexibility are important for engaging in activities and maintaining health and fitness.

Procedure

1. Students warm up for 2-3 minutes, then choose a partner who participates in similar activities outside of class.

2. Give each pair a muscle chart on a clipboard with a pen or pencil. Their task is to discuss and decide what muscle groups they use in this activity or sport. They may circle the names of the muscle groups, but must keep moving.

3. After 3-5 minutes, signal the students to move to a station that stretches a muscle group of their activity. They perform the stretch for 15 to 30 seconds and, on their chart, write the name of the stretch next to the muscle groups used. The students then find another relevant station and continue.

Name: _____   Date: _____

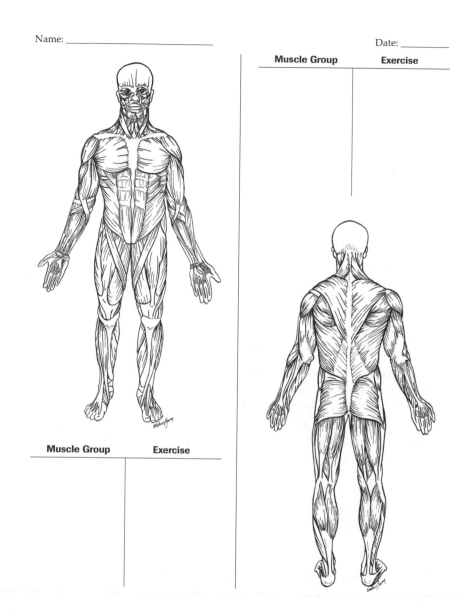

Muscle Group	Exercise

Muscle Group	Exercise

Teaching Hints

Alter (1998) provides an excellent sport-by-sport guide to stretching for reference. Remind students to stretch both sides at each station.

Closure and Assessment

Written and Oral

- Students will write down a muscle group they have not used in this activity and choose a stretch for that muscle group.

Project

- Students select a specific sport or physical activity and list sport- or activity-specific stretches for it.

Extending the Lesson

Have students distinguish (written, orally, or using a videotape) between stretches that emphasize static and dynamic flexibility.

7 | Flexibility Circuit

High School Level

Flexibility is the amount of movement a joint can accomplish, usually described as the **range of motion** around a joint. Maintaining flexibility helps reduce the risk of injury and can improve performance in many activities.

Purpose

Students will demonstrate the different ways to perform stretches for each body part.

Equipment Needed

- Station cards
- Mats

Relationship to National Standards

Physical Education Standard 4: Student achieves and maintains a health-enhancing level of physical fitness—Student demonstrates the skill, knowledge, and desire to monitor and adjust activity levels to meet personal fitness needs.

Health Education Standard 3: Student will demonstrate the ability to practice health-enhancing behaviors and reduce health risks—Student will demonstrate strategies to improve or maintain personal health.

Set Induction

Define flexibility. Remind students that joints are supposed to move, and our bodies can't move efficiently if our joints can't move efficiently.

Procedure

1. Set up a circuit of flexibility exercises. At each station, have the name of the exercise, how to perform the exercise, the benefit of the stretch, and how long to hold it. Each station should have stretches the students are familiar with. Use props to demonstrate different ways to perform the stretch. Examples are as follows:
   - Calves—Place one leg behind the other and stretch the calf.
   - Pectorals—With palms down, extend your arms behind your body.
   - Triceps—Bending one arm behind your neck, grab the elbow and pull gently.
   - Biceps—With palms up, extend your arm out and press it against a wall.
   - Hamstrings—Lie on your back and extend your right leg over your head. Have your left leg straight out. Grab behind the knee and pull back gently.
   - Quadriceps—Lie on your side on the floor. Bend the top knee, then grab the top ankle and pull back, keeping your knees aligned.
2. Divide students into groups for rotation through the stations. Have students warm up using a low-intensity aerobic activity for 3-5 minutes.
3. After the warm-up, rotate students through the stations. Allow enough time at each station for students to practice the stretch on both sides.

Teaching Hints

Refer to books such as Michael Alter's *Sport Stretch* for more stretches and ideas. Remind students to stretch on both sides. Use a video to demonstrate the different exercises. Observe students for proper form during stretches.

Closure and Assessment

Written and Oral

- Have students state the definition of flexibility and one benefit of improving flexibility.

Project

- Students discuss the function of the ligaments, tendons, and muscles, and how they work together to allow flexion and extension.

Extending the Lesson

Have students design a 10-minute stretching video or presentation for a warm-up at the beginning of class.

8 Yoga

High School Level

A regular stretching program improves body mechanics, maintains muscular balance, enhances performance, improves circulation and respiration, and relaxes the body. Several factors contribute to an individual's level of flexibility, including age, activity level, gender, body type, previous injuries, and strength-training level. **Yoga** originated in the Far East, and is a system of exercises that improves flexibility through a variety of slow, long-duration stretches.

Purpose

Students will understand the benefits of stretching through different stretching programs.

Equipment Needed

- Mats
- Video if necessary

Relationship to National Standards

Physical Education Standard 4: Student achieves and maintains a health-enhancing level of physical fitness—Student demonstrates the skill, knowledge, and desire to monitor and adjust activity levels to meet personal needs.

Health Education Standard 3: Student will demonstrate the ability to practice health-enhancing behaviors and reduce health risks—Student will demonstrate strategies to improve or maintain personal health.

Set Induction

Remind students that each individual has a different level of flexibility. Brainstorm factors that might affect an individual's flexibility with the students.

Procedure

1. Either show a yoga video or invite a yoga instructor to teach a session of yoga to the class. This yoga class should provide the basics, including how to breathe while stretching, proper form, basic body mechanics, and exercises for beginners.
2. After a proper warm-up, have students practice the exercises demonstrated in the video or by the instructor.

Teaching Hints

Discuss the benefits of stretching before class and explain that flexibility is individual and influenced by several factors. Each person in the yoga class will feel the stretches differently. Students should progress in the class at their own pace. Make sure the environment is quiet and relaxing for the class.

Closure and Assessment

Written and Oral

- Have the students describe proper breathing while stretching.

Project

- Have students peer-assess and correct two basic yoga stretches.

Extending the Lesson

Have students incorporate one or more yoga stretches into the stretching routine they began developing in Activity 4.

9 | Partner Workouts

High School Level

Frequency refers to how often you should stretch. **Type** refers to the type of flexibility activity—passive (static) or active (dynamic). We recommend stretching before and after intense activity and suggest that you stretch daily for best results.

Purpose

Students will demonstrate their understanding of frequency, intensity, and type.

Equipment Needed

- Mats
- Worksheets with suggested stretches
- Stretching programs and worksheets

Relationship to National Standards

Physical Education Standard 4: Student achieves and maintains a health-enhancing level of physical fitness—Student demonstrates the skill, knowledge, and desire to monitor and adjust activity levels to meet personal fitness needs.

Health Education Standard 3: Student will demonstrate the ability to practice health-enhancing behaviors and reduce health risks—Student will demonstrate strategies to improve or maintain personal health.

Set Induction

Review the definitions of frequency, intensity, and type. Explain that an individual's overall level of activity is a significant factor in determining the frequency, intensity, and type of stretching appropriate for that individual. Brainstorm other significant factors that help determine the appropriate frequency, intensity, and type of stretching.

Procedure

1. Divide students into pairs. Students should design a stretching workout for their partners, keeping the following in mind:
   - The two most important factors influencing stretching are intensity and duration (time). A low-intensity, long-duration stretch favors more lasting effects, whereas a high-intensity, short-duration stretch favors a quick stretch response.
   - Elevated tissue temperature facilitates range of motion.
   - Flexibility is specific; therefore exercises must be specific to each joint and muscle group.
   - Proper alignment for each stretch is crucial in achieving maximum effectiveness.
2. Each student should demonstrate a stretch from the workout plan for his or her partner, then talk him or her through the stretch. The stretch may require the partner's help; if it doesn't, both partners should do the stretch together.

Teaching Hints

Provide a list of stretches that students might want to use. Review the stretching programs the students have designed before the class time. This activity may take two days.

Closure and Assessment

Written and Oral

- Have each student review the stretching plan developed by his or her partner and state which muscle group(s) the plan concentrates on and the best frequency for the plan.

Project

- Have students assess flexibility using the *FITNESSGRAM* flexibility components both before using the stretching plan and after using the stretching plan for three weeks. Compare the results.

Extending the Lesson

Have students write a report about their physical activity plans for the near future and following high school. The report discusses the plans the student has for maintaining satisfactory physical fitness for 10 years after graduation and what barriers the student might encounter.

10 Active/Passive Stretching

High School Level

There are many ways of classifying flexibility exercises, including passive, active-passive, active-assisted, and active. The two most common are **passive** and **active**. **Passive stretching** is a technique in which you are relaxed and make no contribution to the range of motion. Instead, another person or other assistance, such as gravity or special traction equipment, stretches your muscle(s) for you. **Active stretching** is done by yourself, without assistance. Passive stretching allows you to stretch beyond your active range of motion. However, there is an increased risk of soreness and injury if your partner applies the external force incorrectly. Active stretching is best for developing active flexibility, which has a higher correlation to sport achievement than passive flexibility. However, it may be ineffective in the presence of some injuries.

Purpose

Students will learn and demonstrate the different types of passive and active stretches.

Equipment Needed

- Station cards
- Mats

Relationship to National Standards

Physical Education Standard 4: Student achieves and maintains a health-enhancing level of physical fitness—Student demonstrates the skill, knowledge, and desire to monitor and adjust activity levels to meet personal fitness needs.

Health Education Standard 3: Student will demonstrate the ability to practice health-enhancing behaviors and reduce health risks—Student will demonstrate strategies to improve or maintain personal health.

Set Induction

Review the definitions of passive and active stretching. Remind students that proper active stretching involves slow, even motions, not quick, ballistic ones.

Procedure

1. Divide the students into groups of three or four. Set up stretching stations around the gym. One station will be used for passive (partner assisted) stretching. You will supervise this station. All the other stations will be active (by yourself) stretching stations, and each will target a different large-muscle group.

2. After a proper warm-up, send each group of students to a different station.

3. Groups of students independently practice static stretches they've learned in other activities at the static stretching stations. They should peer-assess for proper form, for proper duration, and to ensure that both sides of the body get stretched properly.

4. At the passive stretching station, demonstrate two passive stretches to the group. Then have the students partner up and perform the passive stretches on each other under your close supervision. Here are two sample passive stretches:

   • Hamstring—One student lies on her back on a mat with her legs extended. Her partner grasps one leg and very slowly and smoothly lifts it until the student on the mat can feel the stretch. Hold it for 10-15 seconds, and very slowly and smoothly lower the leg. Repeat with the other leg.

   • Quadriceps—One student lies on his stomach on a mat with his legs extended. His partner grasps one leg and very slowly and smoothly bends it at the knee so the heel of the leg moves toward the back of the leg until the student on the mat can feel the stretch. Hold it for 10-15 seconds, and very slowly and smoothly lower the leg. Repeat with the other leg.

5. Rotate groups after you have worked with each member of the group at your station.

Teaching Hints

Closely monitor students to assure correct form and to avoid injury. Remind students that passive stretching doesn't always need a partner; for example, a doorway can assist in doing a hamstring stretch.

Closure and Assessment

Written and Oral

• Demonstrate a stretch. Have students state whether the stretch is active or passive.

Project

• Have students add one facilitated stretch to their personal stretching plans.

Extending the Lesson

Give students the following scenario: A 20-year-old female wants to start exercising. Her flexibility measurements show a tight back and hamstrings. The doctor has cleared her for exercise, but cautions about frequent back pain. Her goals are to strengthen her back and get into shape. What type of warm-up would you give her? What would you recommend for her stretching routine?

11   Flexibility for You

High School Level

Specificity is using a type of training that is specific to the system you work during the stress of exercise. Duration and type are the two factors that influence flexibility the most.

Purpose

Students will choose and demonstrate specific flexibility exercises for a given sport or activity unit.

Equipment Needed

- Worksheets
- Mats

Relationship to National Standards

Physical Education Standard 4: Student achieves and maintains a health-enhancing level of physical fitness—Student demonstrates the skill, knowledge, and desire to monitor and adjust activity levels to meet personal fitness needs.

Health Education Standard 3: Student will demonstrate the ability to practice health-enhancing behaviors and reduce health risks—Student will demonstrate strategies to improve or maintain personal health.

Set Induction

Ask a student to name his favorite physical activity and state which muscle group is most likely to be strained in that activity. Define specificity, and explain to the students that proper stretching both includes all the major muscle groups and ensures that the muscle groups most used in a particular activity get extra attention.

Procedure

1. During each sport and activity unit, provide a warm-up activity and stretching program for the students. After the students have done the warm-up, they can perform each stretch that benefits that sport or activity unit.

2. Give the students a worksheet that shows the major muscle groups (see appendix). The students will keep a log of each stretch they did for every sport or activity unit throughout the term.

Teaching Hints

Provide a stretching chart that demonstrates the proper forms for the stretches. At the beginning of the units, make sure all students understand the stretches and where they should be feeling the stretch. Have students rotate through the various stretches.

Closure and Assessment

Written and Oral

- Have students pair off. In each pair, one student states a sport or activity, and the other states the muscle group(s) most likely to be stressed during that activity. Students then reverse roles.

Project

- Have students keep a written portfolio of their stretching activities for each sport or activity unit. Have them analyze their own stretching techniques and programs.

Extending the Lesson

Students develop a stretching program for a classmate for a particular sport. The program should include the frequency, intensity, and type of stretch the classmate will perform.

Chapter 11

Body Composition

1 Body Composition Q & A

Middle School Level

Your whole body and all the energy you need is made from the nutrients you get from food. The body uses nutrients to provide energy and structural materials, to regulate growth and maintenance, and to repair its tissues. **Body composition** is the relationship among the body's different kinds of structures, usually expressed as the ratio of lean body mass (muscles, bones, organs, and water) to body fat. To maintain your body composition, you must continually replenish your energy with nutrients from food.

Purpose

The students will learn that a diet including a variety of foods in adequate amounts is necessary for the body to function properly. They will learn the difference between fat mass and lean mass. The students will identify caloric expenditure and caloric intake as key components in maintaining an ideal body composition.

Equipment Needed

- Activity logs
- Jeopardy questions
- Equipment for the activities students choose

Relationship to National Standards

Physical Education Standard 4: Student achieves and maintains a health-enhancing level of physical activity—Student correctly demonstrates activities to improve and maintain muscular strength and endurance, flexibility, cardiorespiratory functioning, and proper body composition.

Health Education Standard 1: Student comprehends the concepts related to health promotion and disease prevention—Student explains the relationship between positive health behaviors and preventing injury, illness, disease, and premature death.

Set Induction

Define body composition, lean mass, and fat mass. Explain to students that body composition depends on more than just dieting, and that an unhealthy body fat ratio can be either very high or very low.

Procedure

1. Make cards that have body composition questions on one side and answers on the back. Some examples of questions for middle school students are:
   - How many calories are in one pound of body fat? 3,500
   - How many calories are in a gram of fat? 9
   - Must you exercise at high intensity to burn fat? No, low intensity works at least as well
   - What instrument is used to measure body fat? Calipers
   - Why is a skinfold measurement a more accurate measure of body fatness than using a height and weight chart? Muscle weighs more than fat

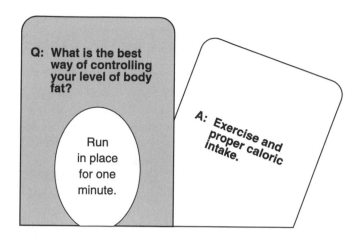

- What percent body fat is too low for males? Less than 10 percent
- What percent body fat is too low for females? Less than 17 percent
- What is the optimal range of body fat for females? 17-32 percent
- What is the optimal range of body fat for males? 10-25 percent
- What is the best way of controlling your level of body fat? Exercise and proper caloric intake
- How many pounds per week can a person lose safely? 1-2

2. Ensure that students warm up before engaging in activities.
3. The cards will have an activity for the students to do. After the student performs the exercise, the partner gives the answer to the body composition question and the student doing the activity answers it as a question. If the answer is correct, place it in a discard pile. If incorrect, put it at the bottom of the pile and do the activity again.

Teaching Hints

Some examples of activities that students can perform are biceps curls, jumping rope, running in place, low back stretch, push-ups, curl-ups, biking, or other strength-training, flexibility, and aerobic endurance training activity. The students should be familiar with the activities first before adding the new education activities. Students can keep a fitness log or journal and write a summary from each station. You can modify activities for age groups.

Closure and Assessment

Written and Oral

- Students tell how intensity and duration of exercise affect calorie expenditure and the resulting body composition.

Project

- Students add cards to the deck with new body composition facts, new activities, or both.

Extending the Lesson

Students keep a body composition and nutrition journal and make at least one entry a week. This entry should focus on how the student's total diet and activity have affected his or her body composition.

2 | Jump Rope Challenges

Middle School Level

Total nutrient needs are greater during adolescence than at any other time of life. The energy you need varies greatly, depending on your current rate of growth, body size, gender, genetics, and physical activity. Iron, calcium, and protein are key nutrients for developing lean body mass and bones during adolescence.

Purpose

Students will understand that normal and natural growth patterns affect nutritional needs and proportions of body fat.

Equipment Needed

- Nutrient cards and descriptions
- Jump ropes

Relationship to National Standards

Physical Education Standard 4: Student achieves and maintains a health-enhancing level of physical fitness—Student uses and applies training principles to improve physical fitness.

Health Education Standard 1: Student comprehends concepts related to health promotion and disease prevention—Student explains how health is influenced by the interaction of body systems.

Set Induction

Explain to students that all foods consumed provide energy for everyday living, energy for growth, and to make body structures during growth. Remind the students that their height and body mass increase very rapidly during adolescence, which requires extra energy and nutrients from food.

Procedure

1. Prepare cards with information on the six nutrient categories: carbohydrates, fats, proteins, vitamins, minerals, and water.
2. Have students choose a card, read the card, and create a jump rope rap or rhyme to perform to the class.

Teaching Hints

Have students write the words to the rap on a station card. The next lesson, students rotate through six stations of jump rope raps and say the rap as they jump.

Closure and Assessment

Written and Oral

- Divide students into small groups. Have one student state one of the jump rope raps without stating the name of the nutrient. The other students in the group then state which nutrient was the subject of the rap.

Project

- Students make "Wanted" posters for "fugitive nutrients" that list the nutrient's benefits and where the nutrient can be found.

Extending the Lesson

Have students prepare at least two "menus" for a nutritionally balanced meal from the school cafeteria, and list the total nutrient values with the menus.

3 Sport Steps

Middle School Level

Nutrition is the study of food and how the body uses it. Carbohydrates, fats, and proteins provide energy (calories) that affect body composition. Other essential nutrients include water, minerals, trace elements, and vitamins to help develop and maintain a healthy body composition. Eating habits affect energy intake, while exercise affects energy output. A healthful diet plan, coupled with physical activity, optimizes health.

Purpose

Students will understand the various nutrients and how they affect growth and development patterns.

Equipment Needed

- Aerobic steps
- Jump ropes
- Food cards
- Menus

Relationship to National Standards

Physical Education Standard 4: Student achieves and maintains a health-enhancing level of physical fitness—Student understands and applies training principles to improve physical fitness.

Health Education Standard 1: Student comprehends concepts related to health promotion and disease prevention—Student explains how health is influenced by the interaction of body systems.

Set Induction

Ask the students how many times during an average week they eat meals away from home, and how many of those meals are fast food. Remind students that diet is the total intake of food over several days, and that eating patterns should include a variety of foods that provide adequate nutrients and an appropriate amount of calories.

Procedure

1. Using menus from fast-food restaurants, cut out 20 or more circles (or other appropriate nutrient shapes from the Food Guide Pyramid). Choose different foods and write the name, total calories, and the number of grams of fat, carbohydrates, and protein in the circle. Place the cards in a container.

2. A student will choose a nutrient and step aerobics movement first, then pick a card from the container. The class will perform the same number of repetitions of the specified movement as the number of grams (for example, a Big Mac has 28 grams fat). Use alternating legs on the movements or do not perform more than eight repetitions on the same leg.

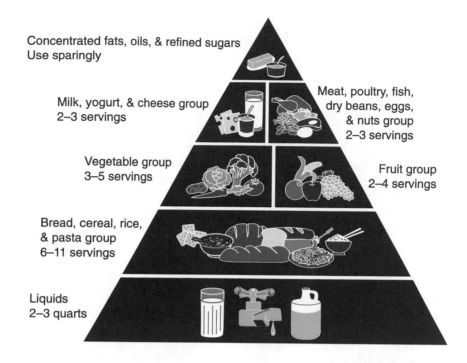

Concentrated fats, oils, & refined sugars
Use sparingly

Milk, yogurt, & cheese group
2–3 servings

Meat, poultry, fish,
dry beans, eggs,
& nuts group
2–3 servings

Vegetable group
3–5 servings

Fruit group
2–4 servings

Bread, cereal, rice,
& pasta group
6–11 servings

Liquids
2–3 quarts

Teaching Hints

Split the class into groups so it is not too large. You can use jump ropes if steps are not available.

Closure and Assessment

Written and Oral

- Students place the food cards from lowest in calorie content to highest in calorie content.

Project

- Have students create typical meals from the food cards.

Extending the Lesson

Using menus from fast food restaurants, design a breakfast, lunch, or dinner meal plan with food that totals less than 30 percent fat content. The meal plan should also state the total amount of protein and carbohydrates.

4 Activity Pyramid Circuit

Middle School Level

Metabolism includes all the reactions the body uses to obtain and spend the energy from food. Your body's top priority in life is to fuel the cells to keep them alive. When you don't eat, the body must turn to other sources for fuel. This may be the energy reserves of carbohydrates and fats in the cells or the proteins in your muscles. When you eat too much over a five to seven day period, the unused energy will be deposited into a "savings account" (usually fat) to be withdrawn later for energy.

Purpose

The students will understand that the calories they consume by activity depend on the duration, intensity, and type of activity. They will learn that calories in must equal calories out to maintain body weight. The students will determine the number of calories they expend and how to calculate the number they use during activity.

Equipment Needed

- Sports equipment for the stations
- Clock
- Jogging area
- Station signs
- Paper and pencil to calculate energy expended

Relationship to National Standards

Physical Education Standard 4: Student achieves and maintains a health-enhancing level of physical fitness—Student understands and applies training principles to improve physical fitness.

Health Education Standard 1: Student comprehends concepts related to health promotion and disease prevention—Student explains how health is influenced by the interaction of body systems.

Set Induction

Explain to students that we measure food energy in calories. When we use more calories than we take in, we lose weight as the body uses its reserves. When we use fewer calories than we take in, we gain weight as the body converts the extra calories to reserves. Review the FITT principles.

Procedure

1. Set up a circuit for six to eight activities of varying intensity, type, and time around the gym. Place a card describing the activity, intensity, type, and time at each station. These cards might list activities like these:
   - Jump rope at high speed for 2 minutes
   - Do 20 curl-ups in no more than 1 minute
   - Jog in place for 3 minutes
   - Do a PACER run for 30 seconds

2. Have the students complete a proper warm-up, including stretching.

3. Rotate students through the stations at even intervals equal to the longest time specified for any station. Instruct students to just keep moving if the activity at their station ends before you rotate the students.

4. Students complete a proper cool-down at the end of this session.

Teaching Hints

With sufficient time remaining, have students go to a thinking area and calculate the amount of energy they expended during each activity and all the activities combined. Provide the students with a list of activity caloric expenditure (see sample in appendix). Make sure the items involve sports, weight training, everyday activities, and so on.

Closure and Assessment

Written and Oral

- Have students list the activities used today in order from highest to lowest intensity.

Project

- Set a calorie-use target and have students create at least three different workouts that meet that target, using just the activities in today's lesson.

Extending the Lesson

Create an outdoor "par course" with activities of varying intensity at six to nine stations.

5   One Thousand Reps

Middle School Level

Nutrition and physical activity go hand in hand. Activity demands carbohydrates and fats as fuel, protein to build and maintain lean tissue, vitamins and minerals to support metabolism and build tissues, and water to help distribute the fuels and heat.

Purpose

Students will understand that physical activity and nutrition are both essential to health-related fitness.

Equipment Needed

- Activity equipment, depending on stations chosen (see Procedure)
- Pen or pencil and paper for each student to record repetitions

Relationship to National Standards

Physical Education Standard 4: Student achieves and maintains a health-enhancing level of physical fitness—Student understands and applies training principles to improve physical fitness.

Health Education Standard 1: Student comprehends concepts related to health promotion and disease prevention—Student explains how health is influenced by the interaction of body systems.

Set Induction

Explain to students that physical activity both burns calories for the energy used up by the activity and requires the body to use nutrients to maintain existing muscle tissue and build new muscle tissue.

Procedure

1. Set up 10 to 12 stations that involve repetitious or timed activities. These might include jump ropes, hula hoops (for rotations), a resistance board for chest presses, a jogging area, a bar for the flexed-arm hang, a basketball and hoop set up for free throws, a soccer ball and cones, aerobics steps, or anything else that involves repeating small activities or maintaining an activity for a given time.

2. After a proper warm-up, divide the students into as many groups as you have stations. Students will keep track of the number of repetitions or number of seconds, as appropriate, for the activity at each station.

3. Rotate between stations every 2 minutes. The objective is to reach 1,000 by adding seconds (for timed activities) to repetitions (for repetitious activities) at the end of the session.

Teaching Hints

For skill-based stations (such as basketball free throws), ensure that students count attempts, not successes, since the goal is activity and not performance. For time-based activities, students should count total time during the rotation; for example, if a student does a 15-second flexed-arm hang and then a 12-second flexed-arm hang, she should score "27" for that station. This activity works especially well when students work with partners.

Closure and Assessment

Written and Oral

- Have students identify which station used the most calories, and which one used the least calories.

Project

- Have students plan their own circuits with their favorite activities. Ensure that the circuits address aerobic endurance, muscular strength and endurance, and flexibility.

Extending the Lesson

- Have students estimate the total number of calories they used in today's activities using the chart in the appendix.

6 Multicultural Food Find

Middle School Level

People decide what to eat, when to eat, and even whether to eat in highly personal ways, often based on behavioral and social motives rather than awareness of nutrition's importance to health. Food choices and practices are often influenced by social interactions, culture, availability, physical appearance, and emotional comfort. A healthy diet includes a balance of nutrients, a variety of foods, and moderation in food choices and servings.

Purpose

Students will understand how society and cultural diversity influence their food choices, which in turn affect their body composition. We will address such issues as advertising, fad diets, and behavioral patterns.

Equipment Needed

- Food pyramid charts
- Food cards
- Stopwatch

Relationship to National Standards

Physical Education Standard 3: Student exhibits a physically active lifestyle—Student describes the relationships between a healthy lifestyle and feeling good.

Health Education Standard 4: Student analyzes the influence of culture, media, technology, and other factors on health—Student describes the influence of cultural beliefs on health behaviors and the use of health services.

Set Induction

Ask students what their favorite foods are. Explain that family traditions and culture will influence many of these preferences, and that there are many ways to fit those preferences into a healthful diet.

Procedure

1. Prepare food cards from all food categories for different ethnic groups, and keep them sorted by ethnic group. Take care to include foods from each ethnic group in your class. For example, an Italian set might include:
   - A fancy dessert, such as *tiramisu*
   - A grilled sausage
   - A plate of spaghetti with tomato sauce
   - A bunch of grapes
   - A small slice of cheese
   - A bowl of minestrone soup
2. Place food cards in the middle of the area, and form four groups in the corners.

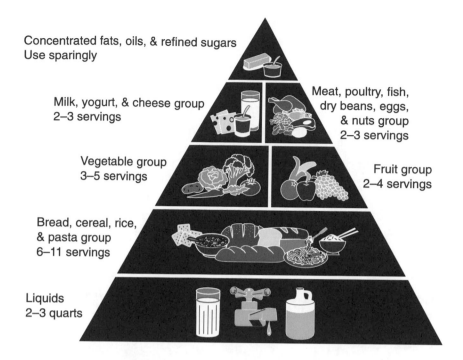

Concentrated fats, oils, & refined sugars
Use sparingly

Milk, yogurt, & cheese group
2–3 servings

Meat, poultry, fish,
dry beans, eggs,
& nuts group
2–3 servings

Vegetable group
3–5 servings

Fruit group
2–4 servings

Bread, cereal, rice,
& pasta group
6–11 servings

Liquids
2–3 quarts

3. Give each group a cultural pyramid as a home base to collect cards. In a relay, each member of the group runs to the center of the circle, collects a card, and places the food in the correct category.

4. Time the groups to see how quickly they can correctly fill their pyramids with foods from the different groups. Repeat the activity with a new culture. Try to beat the score of the last food find.

Teaching Hints

Explain that some cultures do not use dairy products (such as Japan and Korea), so they must obtain calcium from other sources. Remind students that some foods may fit in more than one category (for example, spaghetti with meat sauce includes meat and grains).

Closure and Assessment

Written and Oral

• Select a food category and have students name foods from at least four different cultures that fall in that category.

Project

• Have students take the past week's cafeteria menus and fill a pyramid for each day with what was actually served.

Extending the Lesson

Have students visit local restaurants and grocery stores to determine how their diet is influenced by the diversity in the local community. This may include interviewing managers of chain stores (restaurants and grocery stores) about how sales in their stores are different from those in the entire chain.

7 Quack Attack

Middle School Level

Many people will try anything to lose weight quickly. Consequently products such as "miracle" supplements, diet pills, and fad diets have become popular. Starvation diets and diet pills may show a quick weight loss on the scale, but in the end, most people gain the weight back plus some more. Some people also use steroids and so-called muscle-building supplements to develop muscular mass and definition. These products can harm or kill users. Using steroids has severe side effects, including heart, lung, and kidney problems.

Purpose

Students will identify the difference between sound nutritional practices and fad diets and will identify misleading information about nutrition.

Equipment Needed

- Fact cards
- Recording sheets
- Fiction cards

Relationship to National Standards

Physical Education Standard 3: Student exhibits a physically active lifestyle—Student describes the relationships between a healthy lifestyle and feeling good.

Health Education Standard 1: Student comprehends concepts related to health promotion and disease prevention—Student explains how health is influenced by the interaction of body systems.

Set Induction

Explain that a healthful diet should have all the nutrients your body needs to maintain fitness. Remind the students that specific supplements are most useful when the diet is deficient in particular nutrients.

Procedure

1. Set up nutritional information stations as a par course, using the fact cards.
2. Divide the students into groups of 4-6. Give each group nutrition myths or quackery statements.
3. Students jog to information stations to learn the facts so they can correct the misleading information. Have the students write the facts on a recording sheet.

Teaching Hints

Here are some sample myths:

- Never drink fluids before or during competition
- Honey is more nutritious than sugar
- Dieting by itself is an effective way to lose fat
- When you stop working out, your muscles turn to fat
- You need protein supplements if you are going to weight train

Closure and Assessment

Written and Oral

- Have each group of students state a health benefit of fitness and one (or more) food groups closely related to that benefit.

Project

- Have students find a nutritional advertisement in a magazine and analyze the credibility of its claims.

Extending the Lesson

Divide the students into small groups. Have each group interview a different nutritional expert about fad diets and appropriate weight-loss programs.

8 The Challenge

High School Level

Body composition includes lean and fat body components. Lean body mass is dense and heavy and is made up of muscles, bones, organs, blood, and body fluids. Fat tissue is less dense and lighter than lean tissue. Fat is distributed under the skin, around body organs, and in the muscle tissue. To maintain a healthy body composition, you must perform cardiovascular, muscular strength and endurance, and flexibility exercises.

Purpose

Students will evaluate the appropriate balance of fat and lean body tissue for optimum function of the body and its systems.

Equipment Needed

- Skinfold calipers
- Hand weights or any other resistance (sandbags, etc.)
- Worksheets
- Towels or pillows for padding

Relationship to National Standards

Physical Education Standard 4: Student achieves and maintains a health-enhancing level of physical fitness—Student demonstrates the skill and knowledge to monitor body composition to meet personal needs.

Health Education Standard 1: Student comprehends concepts related to health promotion and disease prevention—Student describes how to delay onset and reduce risks of potential health problems during adulthood.

Set Induction

Define lean body mass and fat tissue. Review the need to develop and maintain an appropriate proportion of lean body mass to fat tissue. Remind students that both diet and physical activity have significant impact on body composition.

Procedure

1. Set up a circuit with cardiovascular endurance, muscular strength and endurance, and flexibility activities. At each station, provide various weights for the student to carry while performing the activity.
2. Have students perform the *FITNESSGRAM* skinfold caliper or body mass index test.
3. After a proper warm-up, rotate the students through the stations. Have them try the activities at the stations both with and without the extra weights. The students should write the extra weight carried, how they felt, and their heart rates at each station.

Teaching Hints

Choose activities that are low impact to avoid injury. Weight belts with sandbags in them give added weight for some activities. On flexibility exercises, use towels or pillows to limit the range of motion while performing the stretch.

Closure and Assessment

Written and Oral

- Ask students to state why two individuals with the same height and similar weight can have significantly different body compositions.

Project

- Provide a *FITNESSGRAM* report for each student. Have each student write a one-paragraph plan for either maintaining body composition in the healthy range or bringing body composition into the healthy range, depending on their initial score. File the plan in the student portfolio for review in four to six weeks.

Extending the Lesson

Have students research the different body composition measurement techniques.

9 Step Your Way to Health

High School Level

The body needs a **healthy amount of fat** to protect vital organs, keep warm, use vitamins effectively, and provide energy. Too much or too little fat can be dangerous to your health. Inactive lifestyles and poor nutrition practices can lead to diseases such as obesity, diabetes, heart disease, cancer, anorexia, or bulimia. To maintain a healthy body composition, you must perform cardiovascular, muscular strength and endurance, and flexibility exercises.

Purpose

Students will understand the relationship of body composition to health and the components of fitness. Students will work on their cardiovascular and muscular endurance, emphasizing motivation.

Equipment Needed

- Aerobic steps
- Weights or bands

Relationship to National Standards

Physical Education Standard 4: Student achieves and maintains a health-enhancing level of physical fitness—Student demonstrates the skill and knowledge to monitor body composition for meeting personal needs.

Health Education Standard 1: Student comprehends concepts related to health promotion and disease prevention—Student analyzes how behavior can impact health maintenance and disease prevention.

Set Induction

Review the definitions of fat tissue and lean body mass. Brainstorm possible health effects of too much body fat with students, then repeat with too little body fat.

Procedure

1. Design a step aerobics class that has 8 blocks, alternating 4 aerobic endurance blocks with 4 muscular strength and endurance blocks. Each block should last 3 minutes. Each block should include a variety of movements. One possible sequence of blocks is:
   - Basic stepping (aerobic endurance)
   - Squat (muscular strength and endurance)
   - Stepping and turning (aerobic endurance)
   - Lateral shoulder raise (muscular strength and endurance)
   - Basic stepping (aerobic endurance)
   - Shoulder press and upright raise (muscular strength and endurance)
   - Stepping and extending (aerobic endurance)
   - Push-ups on the step (muscular strength and endurance)

2. After a proper warm-up, lead the students through the activity. This should take 24 minutes. After completing the activity, ensure that you and the students perform a proper cool-down.

Teaching Hints

Use any step aerobic combination or a step video, and teach the difficult moves before class. If the class is advanced, have students design a routine and teach it to the class. Explain to students that, just as each step routine builds on the previous one, your nutrition and physical activity trends build to create your body composition.

Closure and Assessment

Written and Oral

- List a variety of body composition-related health disorders. Have students state whether the disorder comes from too much body fat, too little body fat, or other nutritional problems.

Project

- Have students review their body composition paragraphs from Activity 8. After this review, have students include a step routine into their plans.

Extending the Lesson

Discuss our societal obsession with slenderness. Remind students of health problems, such as eating disorders, that have come to light since this obsession began.

10 Personal Fitness Challenge

High School Level

Total nutrient needs vary at different stages of maturation. Heredity, metabolism, early fatness, maturation, age, gender, nutrition, and physical activity are factors that affect body composition, shape, type, and size. We can control some of these influences but others are genetic.

Purpose

Students will understand the differences in body types (endomorph, ectomorph, mesomorph) and identify their own growth and developmental influences.

Equipment Needed

- Worksheets for the challenge
- Caloric expenditure chart for activities

Relationship to National Standards

Physical Education Standard 4: Student achieves and maintains a health-enhancing level of physical fitness—Student designs a personal fitness program.

Health Education Standard 3: Student demonstrates the ability to practice health-enhancing behaviors and reduce health risks—Student develops strategies to improve or maintain personal, family, and community health.

Set Induction

Define ectomorph, endomorph, and mesomorph. Remind students that body types are individual, and that no one body type is necessarily better than any other. Review the concepts of goal setting.

Procedure

1. Using the worksheet in the appendix as a guide, have students create a fitness plan that focuses on achieving a healthy proportion of lean body mass to fat tissue. The fitness plans should include:
   - A proper warm-up and cool-down, including stretching
   - Aerobic endurance exercises
   - Muscular strength and endurance exercises
2. After the students complete their fitness plans, have the students practice the initial workout on the plan.
3. Remind students that a complete fitness plan will also include a healthful diet appropriate to the individual's needs and activities.

Teaching Hints

Guide the students in realistic goal setting, keeping in mind the growth and developmental influences on their bodies. Students must be comfortable with keeping records of body weight as well as calorie intake and usage. Provide the students with a worksheet outlining their personal fitness goal-setting action plan.

Closure and Assessment

Written and Oral

- Have students name a factor that contributes to body composition and state whether that factor is controllable or uncontrollable.

Project

- Have each student privately reflect on his or her body type and write a two paragraph statement. The first paragraph should define the student's body type and uncontrollable factors that influence his or her body composition. The second paragraph should discuss how the student will deal with controllable factors to meet his or her fitness goals. Ensure that these paragraphs are kept between you and the individual student.

Extending the Lesson

- Have each student develop a fitness notebook that includes the following:
  - Health-related fitness results
  - Goal-setting worksheet
  - Personal fitness plan
  - Activity plan
- Have students research and report on five health-related fitness articles from five different credible resources. They should read articles about flexibility, muscular strength and endurance, cardiovascular fitness, and how they influence weight control.

11 Estimating Energy Needs

High School Level

Metabolism is the process the body uses to break down nutrients to yield energy and to create body structures. Burning fats, carbohydrates, and proteins releases heat, water, and carbon dioxide. The body's metabolism is regulated by energy needs. Thus, the energy from food supports every activity from quiet thought to vigorous activity.

Purpose

Students will understand that the FITT principles—frequency, intensity, time, and type—progression, and specificity all help determine caloric expenditure and nutritional needs during activity. The students will be able to explain the combined use of exercise and diet as a method for weight control versus diet or exercise alone.

Equipment Needed

- Station activity cards
- Station equipment
- Caloric expenditure chart
- Worksheet with questions (see step 3 of Procedure below)
- Daily energy needs worksheet

Relationship to National Standards

Physical Education Standard 3: Student exhibits a physically active lifestyle—Student understands how his or her activity participation patterns may change throughout life and has some strategies to deal with those changes.

Health Education Standard 1: Student comprehends concepts related to health promotion and disease prevention—Student explains the impact of personal health behaviors on how body systems function.

Set Induction

Define metabolism. The body at rest requires energy, usually called the resting metabolic rate (RMR). Explain that even quiet activities, such as reading a book, use some energy. Remind students that the energy used in an activity depends on both the intensity (how much energy is required at any one moment) and duration of the activity.

Procedure

1. Set up a workout circuit. Each station has an activity of varying intensity, time, and duration. Set up one additional "thinking" station with a sample calorie expenditure chart (see appendix), paper, pens or pencils, and several questions (see step 3).
2. Begin with a proper warm-up. Students then begin to rotate through the different stations, performing each activity indicated. Students should monitor their heart rates at each station to ensure they are exercising in the target zone.

3. When a student completes the activity stations, he or she goes to the "thinking" station to answer the questions. Sample questions might include:
   - How many calories does a 150-pound person expend playing soccer for 30 minutes?
   - Which person will burn more calories taking a moderate aerobics class for 30 minutes: a 120-pound woman or a 150-pound man?
   - How many calories did you expend at (specify one of the stations in the circuit)?

Teaching Hints

Provide approximately 5 to 10 questions varying in difficulty for the end of the activity. Remind students to show their calculations to reinforce the role of both intensity and duration in determining total energy expenditure.

Closure and Assessment

Written and Oral

- The students' answers to the questions are an excellent written assessment.

Project

- Have students choose a favorite sport or activity. Have them calculate the energy expenditure of one performer for one session, allowing for periods of inactivity during the session (for example, a football quarterback is not on the field for the entire 60 minutes).

Extending the Lesson

Students develop a fitness program for a partner based on daily estimated caloric expenditure and activity level. This fitness program should be to maintain weight and involve all fitness components (aerobic endurance, muscular strength and endurance, flexibility, and body composition).

12 Cognitive Scavenger Hunt

High School Level

Engaging in regular physical activity is essential to maintaining desired body composition. The **resting metabolic rate (RMR)** is how much energy the body burns while at rest. Physical activity increases RMR, which in turn reduces levels of body fat (influencing physical appearance and health) by using body fat for energy. Physical activity also affects muscle tone and total weight. The number of calories you burn is based on the amount of weight you move, the distance you move it, and the duration of your effort. Exercise over time will increase your basal metabolic rate. Maintaining healthy body composition requires a lifetime of continuous activity and appropriate eating habits.

Purpose

Students will understand that diet and exercise work together to provide a healthy body.

Equipment Needed

- Station cards
- Stopwatch

Relationship to National Standards

Physical Education Standard 4: Student achieves and maintains a health-enhancing level of physical fitness—Student demonstrates the skill, knowledge, and desire to monitor and adjust activity levels to meet personal fitness needs.

Health Education Standard 3: Student demonstrates the ability to practice health-enhancing behaviors and reduce health risks—Student develops strategies to improve or maintain personal, family, and community health.

Set Induction

Define RMR. Explain that the body uses energy even when sleeping, and that a higher RMR uses more fat from the body's fat stores.

Procedure

1. Set up a par course or a fitness scavenger hunt. Stations should present problems for the groups to solve in the area of health and body composition, exercise, and weight control. Here are some sample problems:
   - Historically, nutritionists have thought that losing one pound of body weight requires consuming about 3,500 calories less than you use. (This number actually depends upon several factors, including level of activity.) How much must you raise your RMR to lose one pound in one week without changing your food intake or overall activity level?
   - Bob's RMR is 100 calories/hour, and Keshawn's RMR is 110 calories/hour. Their overall activity levels are the same. Both students want to maintain their current weights. How much more food can Keshawn eat in an average day than Bob without gaining weight?

- Fats provide 9 calories per gram, while carbohydrates and proteins provide 4 calories per gram. If a healthy diet obtains 30 percent or less of its calories from fat, what is the maximum number of grams of fat that an individual who consumes 2,000 calories a day should consume in a week?

- Losing one pound requires consuming about 3,500 calories less than you use. Melissa, who weighs 130 pounds, wants to lose 3 pounds in the next month without changing her food intake. She likes to jog at a pace of 9 minutes per mile (just under 7 miles an hour), which burns about 330 calories in an hour. How many hours must she jog this month to meet her weight-loss goal?

2. Divide the class into teams of six students. Each team must complete the activity as a group.

3. Members of the winning team will be able to give the most correct answers to the problems presented. Students may spend no more than one minute at each station.

Teaching Hints

Make sure each group has a watch. Many watches have a countdown feature that the student can set for one minute.

Closure and Assessment

Written and Oral

- Ask students to define the effect of physical activity on RMR.

Project

- Have the students develop three different plans to lose three pounds in one month: one that relies only on eating less, one that relies only on increasing activity, and one that combines eating less with increasing activity.

Extending the Lesson

Have students go to a store or library and look at current magazines. Have them pick several popular magazines and write down the name of the magazine, the number of weight-loss articles in that issue, and the target audience for the magazine. Have the students report their findings to the class. Open a class discussion by asking the students to explain what their findings tell us about what Americans think about weight and weight control.

13 Spot the Fallacy

High School Level

This material relates consumer and societal issues to body composition.

Purpose

The students will differentiate among fact, fad, quackery, and fallacies related to fitness and nutrition. They will determine the validity of marketing claims promoting fitness products and services and will identify consumer issues related to selection, purchase, care, and maintenance of personal fitness equipment. The students will identify dangers associated with using performance enhancing drugs (PEDs).

Equipment Needed

- Station cards (one for each pair of students in the class)
- Questions
- Worksheets
- Equipment for stations

Relationship to National Standards

Physical Education Standard 4: Student achieves and maintains a health-enhancing level of physical fitness—Student demonstrates the skill, knowledge, and desire to monitor and adjust activity levels to meet personal fitness needs.

Health Education Standard 2: Student demonstrates the ability to access valid health information and health-promoting products and services—Student evaluates the validity of health information, products, and services.

Set Induction

Ask students to describe an advertisement that they have seen recently for a food product or nutritional supplement. Did the advertisement make any health claims? What did the advertisement imply about the product? Present one or two examples of misleading advertising and ask the same questions.

Procedure

1. Set up a circuit for pairs of students. At each station, provide cards with facts, fads, quackery, and fallacies related to health. Each card should have a question, answer, and activity. Activities should range across aerobic endurance, muscular strength and endurance, and flexibility. Some examples:

   • "True or False: When you do not do muscular strength and endurance exercises, your muscles turn to fat." True = 10 push-ups; False = 15 push-ups

   • "True or False: Diets that depend on a special food are effective weight-loss methods for most people." True = 3 minutes of step aerobics; False = 2 minutes of step aerobics.

   • "True or False: The lower your body fat, the better your health." True = 30 curl-ups; False = 20 curl-ups.

2. After a proper warm-up, divide the students into pairs and send them around to the different stations. At each station, one partner asks the question on the card. The other partner gives his or her answer. The students then do the activity specified on the card for that answer.

3. Rotate between stations every 3 minutes, reminding the students to trade roles with each station.

Teaching Hints

Have students do research on fads, quackery, and fallacies related to health. Ensure questions emphasize weight loss and weight gain at reasonable, slow rates; why obesity is dangerous; theories on vitamins; and so on. Ensure that questions have easy-to-verify answers.

Closure and Assessment

Written and Oral

• Have students gather and discuss the answers to the questions.

Project

• Have each student write a "quack" ad for a new diet. Have students exchange articles and find the facts, the myths, and the misleading statements in each.

Extending the Lesson

Have students create a resource file on fitness products, nutritional supplements, and other supposed health-enhancing products.

14   Lifelong Fitness Plan

High School Level

Overall health is influenced by many aspects of our lifestyles, such as fitness level; activity frequency, intensity, duration, and type; nutrition; emotional well-being; family history; smoking and drug and alcohol use; human values; and self-care. A **fitness plan** considers all of these factors to improve an individual's health-related fitness.

Purpose

Students will understand how to create a lifelong fitness plan based on their lifestyle and the knowledge they've obtained in this program.

Equipment Needed

- Fitness plan and goal-setting worksheets (see appendix)
- Pens and pencils
- Equipment for the activities in the plans students will design

Relationship to National Standards

Physical Education Standard 4: Student achieves and maintains a health-enhancing level of physical fitness—Student designs a personal fitness program.

Health Education Standard 3: Student demonstrates the ability to practice health-enhancing behaviors and reduce health risks—Student develops strategies to improve or maintain personal, family, and community health.

Set Induction

Review the goal-setting process. Remind students that a good plan will include both short- and long-term goals.

Procedure

1. Have students create a fitness notebook. This notebook is based on their personal interests only, whether sport-related or general activity. Students must include the following components in their plans.
   - Discussion of what their ultimate goal will be, using the goal-setting worksheet in the appendix.
   - An assessment of their current fitness level. A *FITNESSGRAM* report is helpful with this.
   - Several copies of the workout plan worksheet.
   - Several blank pages for journaling.
2. Students create a fitness plan using the first workout plan worksheet in their notebooks.
3. After creating the fitness plans, students peer-assess the fitness plans and incorporate the assessment into the plans. This should include:
   - Determining how the fitness plan will help meet an individual's goals.
   - Discussing the role of diet in attaining the individual's goals.

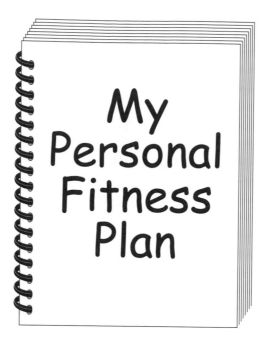

4. Repeat this activity every six to eight weeks. Encourage students to review and revise the plans on their own during school vacations.

Teaching Hints

Remind students that no one plan is perfect. The best plan is one that the student can complete because it is enjoyable, realistic, and likely to lead to achieving the goal. You should also participate in the process with your students by presenting your own fitness plan and inviting comments from students.

Closure and Assessment

Written and Oral

- Have each student state one thing he or she learned through the peer assessment.

Project

- Encourage students to make notebooks for each member of their families and go through the planning, assessment, and review process with them.

Extending the Lesson

Have students analyze their diet plans using diet analysis software (available through some schools, many public health departments, and on the Internet). Does the software's analysis point out any areas for changing the plans? Does the analysis consider the students' individual circumstances, such as cultural food preferences?

References

Alter, Michael J. 1998. *Sport Stretch*. 2nd ed. Champaign, IL: Human Kinetics.

Baechle, Thomas R., and Barney Groves. 1998, 1994. *Weight Training: Steps to Success*. Champaign, IL: Human Kinetics.

Biddle, Stuart, and Marios Goudas. 1996. "Analysis of Children's Physical Activity and Its Association With Adult Encouragement and Social Cognitive Values." *Journal of School Health* 66(2):75-78.

Bouchard, Claude, et al., eds. 1993. *Physical Activity, Fitness, and Health Consensus Statement*. Champaign, IL: Human Kinetics.

Centers for Disease Control (CDC). 1999. *Promoting Physical Activity: A Guide for Community Action*. Champaign, IL: Human Kinetics.

Cheung, Lilian W.Y., and Julius B. Richmond, eds. 1995. *Child Health, Nutrition, and Physical Activity*. Champaign, IL: Human Kinetics.

Corbin, Charles B. 1987. "Physical Fitness in the K-12 Curriculum: Some Defensible Solutions to Perennial Problems." *Journal of Physical Education, Recreation and Dance* 58(7):49-54.

Corbin, Charles B., and R. Lindsey. 1997. *Fitness for Life*. 4th ed. Glenview, IL: Scott, Foresman.

Council on Physical Education for Children (COPEC). 1992. *Developmentally Appropriate Physical Education Practices for Children*. Reston, VA: National Association for Sport and Physical Education (NASPE).

Craft, Diane H. 1996. "A Focus on Inclusion in Physical Education." In *Physical Education Sourcebook,* ed. Betty F. Hennessy. Champaign, IL: Human Kinetics.

Davison, Bev. 1998. *Creative Physical Activities and Equipment*. Champaign, IL: Human Kinetics.

Desmond, Sharon M., et al. 1986. "The Etiology of Adolescents' Perceptions of Their Weight." *Journal of Youth & Adolescence* 15(6):461-474.

Fleck, Steven J., and William J. Kraemer. 1997. *Designing Resistance Training Programs*. 2nd ed. Champaign, IL: Human Kinetics.

Graham, George. 1992. *Teaching Children Physical Education: Becoming a Master Teacher*. Champaign, IL: Human Kinetics.

Harris, Jo, and Jill Elbourn. 1997. *Teaching Health-Related Exercise at Key Stages 1 and 2*. Champaign, IL: Human Kinetics.

Hennessy, Betty F., ed. 1996. *Physical Education Sourcebook*. Champaign, IL: Human Kinetics.

Hichwa, John. 1998. *Right Fielders Are People Too: An Inclusive Approach to Teaching Middle School Physical Education*. Champaign, IL: Human Kinetics.

Hill, James O., and John C. Peters. 1998. "Environmental Contributions to the Obesity Epidemic." *Science* 280 (May 29):1371-74.

Hinson, Curt. 1995. *Fitness for Children*. Champaign, IL: Human Kinetics.

Hopper, Christine J., et al. 1997. *Health-Related Fitness for Grades 5 and 6*. Champaign, IL: Human Kinetics.

————. 1995. *Teaching for Outcomes in Elementary Physical Education*. Champaign, IL: Human Kinetics.

Human Kinetics. 1998. *Active Youth: Ideas for Implementing CDC Physical Activity Promotion Guidelines*. Champaign, IL: Human Kinetics.

Individuals With Disabilities Education Act. 20 U.S.C. §§ 1400 *et seq.*, 84 Stat. 175, Pub. L. 91-230 (1970 as amended).

Kraemer, William J., and Steven J. Fleck. 1993. *Strength Training for Young Athletes*. Champaign, IL: Human Kinetics.

Lavay, Barry W., et al. 1997. *Positive Behavior Management Strategies for Physical Educators*. Champaign, IL: Human Kinetics.

Leadly, Kathleen. 1994. "Physical Education Homework." *Teaching Elementary Physical Education* (March):13.

McAtee, Robert E. 1999. *Facilitated Stretching*. 2nd ed. Champaign, IL: Human Kinetics.

McGinnis, J.M., and W.H. Foege. 1993. "Actual Causes of Death in the United States." *JAMA* 270(18):2207-12.

McSwegin, P.J., et al. 1989. "Fitting in Fitness." *Journal of Physical Education, Recreation and Dance* 60(1):30-45.

Melograno, Vincent J. 1998. *Professional and Student Portfolios for Physical Education*. Champaign, IL: Human Kinetics.

Mosston, Muska, and Sara Ashworth. 1994. *Teaching Physical Education*. 4th ed. New York: Macmillan.

————. 1990. *The Spectrum of Teaching Styles: From Command to Discovery*. New York: Longman.

National Association for Sport and Physical Education (NASPE). 1995, 1992. *Moving Into the Future: National Standards for Physical Education, a Guide to Content and Assessment*. St. Louis: Mosby.

National Consortium for Physical Education and Recreation for Individuals With Disabilities (NCPERID). 1995. *Adapted Physical Education National Standards*. Champaign, IL: Human Kinetics.

Nieman, David C. 1998. *The Exercise-Health Connection*. Champaign, IL: Human Kinetics.

Ormrod, J.E. 1995. *Educational Psychology Principles and Applications*. Columbus, OH: Merrill.

Paffenbarger, Ralph S., Jr., and Eric Olsen. 1996. *LifeFit: An Effective Exercise Program for Optimal Health and a Longer Life*. Champaign, IL: Human Kinetics.

Pate, Russell R., and Richard C. Hohn. 1994. *Health and Fitness Through Physical Education*. Champaign, IL: Human Kinetics.

Raffini, James P. 1993. *Winners Without Losers: Structures and Strategies for Increasing Student Motivation to Learn*. Needham Heights, MA: Allyn & Bacon.

Rainey, Don L., and Tinker D. Murray. 1997. *Foundations of Personal Fitness: Any Body Can... Be Fit!* St. Paul, MN: West.

Ratliffe, Thomas, and Laraine M. Ratliffe. 1994. *Teaching Children Fitness: Becoming a Master Teacher*. Champaign, IL: Human Kinetics.

Rink, Judith R., and Larry D. Hensley. 1996. "Assessment in the School Physical Education Program." In *Physical Education Sourcebook*, ed. Betty F. Hennessy, 39-55. Champaign, IL: Human Kinetics.

Rowland, Thomas W. 1990. *Exercise and Children's Health*. Champaign, IL: Human Kinetics.

Safrit, Margaret J. 1995. *Complete Guide to Youth Fitness Testing*. Champaign, IL: Human Kinetics.

Sallis, James F. 1991. "Self-Report Measures of Children's Physical Activity." *Journal of School Health* 61(5):215-219.

Saltman, Paul, Joel Gurin, and Ira Mothner. 1993. *The University of California at San Diego Nutrition Book*. Boston: Little, Brown.

Schiemer, Suzanne. 1996. "A Positive Learning Experience: Self-Assessment Sheets Let Students Take an Active Role in Learning." *Teaching Elementary Physical Education* (March):4-6.

Sharkey, Brian J. 1997. *Fitness and Health*. 4th ed. Champaign, IL: Human Kinetics.

Siedentop, Daryl. 1991. *Developing Teaching Skills in Physical Education*. 3rd ed. Mountain View, CA: Mayfield.

Strand, Bradford N., et al. 1997. *Fitness Education: Teaching Concepts-Based Fitness in the Schools*. Scottsdale, AZ: Gorsuch Scarisbrick.

Surgeon General of the United States. 1996. *Physical Activity and Health at a Glance: A Report of the Surgeon General*. Washington, DC: U.S. Government Printing Office.

Taubes, Gary. 1998. "As Obesity Rates Rise, Experts Struggle to Explain Why." *Science* 280 (May 29):1367-68.

Virgilio, Stephen J. 1997. *Fitness Education for Children*. Champaign, IL: Human Kinetics.

Walsh, B. Timothy, and Michael J. Devlin. 1998. "Eating Disorders: Progress and Problems." *Science* 280 (May 29):1387-90.

Wickelgren, Ingrid. 1998. "Obesity: How Big a Problem?" *Science* 280 (May 29):1364-67.

Appendix

Worksheets

FITNESSGRAM

Jane Marie Jogger
FITNESSGRAM Jr. High

Instructor Susan Anderson   **Grade** 8   **Age** 14

	Test Date	Height	Weight
Past:	05/06/97	5' 2"	147
Current:	10/02/98	5' 2"	145

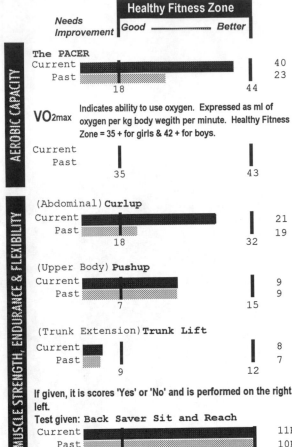

AEROBIC CAPACITY

Healthy Fitness Zone
Needs Improvement | Good —————— Better

The PACER
Current — 40
Past 18 — 44 — 23

VO2max Indicates ability to use oxygen. Expressed as ml of oxygen per kg body weigth per minute. Healthy Fitness Zone = 35 + for girls & 42 + for boys.
Current
Past 35 — 43

MUSCLE STRENGTH, ENDURANCE & FLEXIBILITY

(Abdominal) Curlup
Current — 21
Past 18 — 32 — 19

(Upper Body) Pushup
Current — 9
Past 7 — 15 — 9

(Trunk Extension) Trunk Lift
Current — 8
Past 9 — 12 — 7

If given, it is scores 'Yes' or 'No' and is performed on the right and left.
Test given: Back Saver Sit and Reach
Current — 11R 11L
Past 10 — 10 — 10R 11L

BODY COMPOSITION

Percent Body Fat
Current — 34.28
Past 32 — 13 — 35.5

Janie, your scores on four of six test items were in or above the Healthy Fitness Zone. You are also doing flexibility exercises. However, you need to participate in aerobic activities most every day and do some strength exercises.

Although your aerobic capacity is in the Healthy Fitness Zone now, you are not doing enough physical activity. Try to participate in moderate or vigorous aerobic activities 30 to 60 minutes at least five days each week to maintain your fitness.

Janie, if you will do physical activity most days, you may see an improvement in your body composition. Also, eat a healthy diet including more fruits and vegetables and fewer fats and sugars. Improving body composition may help improve other fitness scores.

Your trunk extensions may be improved by doing repeated trunk lifts in a slow, controlled manner. Do these exercises 3 to 5 days each week.

Your abdominal and upper body strength are both in the Healthy Fitness Zone. To maintain your fitness, you should begin doing strength activities that include resistance exercises for each of these areas. Abdominal exercises should be done 3 to 5 days each week. Strength activities for other parts of the body should be done 2 to 3 days each week.

Janie, your flexibility is in the Healthy Fitness Zone. To maintain your fitness, continue to stretch 20-30 seconds. Don't forget that you need to stretch all areas of the body.

Activity Questions

Days

On how many of the past 7 days did you particpate in physical activity for a total of 30-60 minutes, or more, over the course of a day? **3**

On how many of the past 7 days did you do exercises to strengthen or tone your muscles? **0**

On how many of the past 7 days did you do stretching exercises to loosen up or relax your muscles? **3**

To be healthy and fit it is important to do some physical activity almost everyday. Aerobic exercise is good for your heart and and body composition. Strength and flexibility exercise are good for your muscles and joints. Try to do some more aerobic and strength exercise to keep your body fit.

Activity Goals Contract

Week of _____   My plans are to do:

	Activity I plan to do	Time of day	Friend(s) who will be active with me
Monday			
Tuesday			
Wednesday			
Thursday			
Friday			
Saturday			
Sunday			

Student:_____   Date:_____   Teacher:_____

Aerobic Activity Frequency Log

Name: _____ Date begun: _____

	Sun	Mon	Tue	Wed	Thu	Fri	Sat	Total
Week 1 (beginning _____)								
Week 2 (beginning _____)								
Week 3 (beginning _____)								
Week 4 (beginning _____)								
Week 5 (beginning _____)								
Week 6 (beginning _____)								
Week 7 (beginning _____)								

Using this worksheet: Monitor your heart rate during physical activity. You earn one point for each 10 minute session that your heart rate stays in the aerobic fitness training zone. At the end of each day, write the number of points you earned that day in the box.

Borg Ratings of Perceived Exertion Scale

6	No exertion at all
7	Extremely light
8	
9	Very light
10	
11	Light
12	
13	Somewhat hard
14	
15	Hard (heavy)
16	
17	Very hard
18	
19	Extremely hard
20	Maximal exertion

© Gunnar Borg, 1970, 1985, 1994, 1998.

Calories Expended by Some Common Activities

Activity	Duration to expend 150 calories (minutes)	Intensity
Volleyball (recreational)	43	Moderate
Walking at 3 mph (20 min/mile)	37	Moderate
Walking at 4 mph (15 min/mile)	32	Moderate
Table tennis	32	Moderate
Raking leaves	32	Moderate
Social dancing	29	Moderate
Mowing the lawn (powered push mower)	29	Moderate
Jogging at 5 mph (12 min/mile)	18	High
Field hockey	16	High
Running at 6 mph (10 min/mile)	13	Very high

Note: All calculations are based on a 155-lb individual.

Surgeon General of the United States. 1996. *Physical Activity and Health*.

Fitness Goals Contract

To improve my personal fitness level, I, with the help of my teacher, have set the following fitness goals. I will participate in the activities outlined in this plan to achieve improved physical fitness. Based on my current level of fitness, I believe that these goals are reasonable.

Fitness component test item Circle appropriate item	Score Date: _____	My goal	Activities to improve physical fitness	Follow-up score Date: _____
Aerobic Fitness *One-mile walk/run* *The PACER*				
Body Composition *Percent body fat* *Body mass index*				
Muscular Strength and Endurance & Flexibility *Curl-up*				
Trunk lift				
Push-ups *Modified pull-ups* *Pull-ups* *Flexed-arm hang*				
Back-saver sit-and-reach *Shoulder stretch*				

Student: _____ Date: _____ Teacher: _____

Fitness Workout Plan

Name: _____   Date: _____

Week Beginning:

Component	Activity	Mon	Tue	Wed	Thu	Fri	Weekend
	Warm-up						
Aerobic Fitness							
Muscular Strength & Endurance							
Flexibility							
Body Composition							
	Cool-down						

Muscle-Maker Menu

Name: _____

Date: _____

Muscle Group	Exercise

Muscle Group	Exercise

Muscular Strength and Endurance Training Log

Name: _____   Date: _____

Monday	Week 1	Week 2	Week 3	Week 4	Week 5	Week 6
	2 × 5	2 × 5	2 × 5	2 × 5	2 × 5	2 × 5
	2 × 5	2 × 5	2 × 5	2 × 5	2 × 5	2 × 5
	2 × 10	2 × 10	2 × 10	2 × 10	2 × 10	2 × 10
	2 × 5	2 × 5	2 × 5	2 × 5	2 × 5	2 × 5
	2 × 10	2 × 10	2 × 10	2 × 10	2 × 10	2 × 10
	2 × 5	2 × 5	2 × 5	2 × 5	2 × 5	2 × 5
	2 × 10	2 × 10	2 × 10	2 × 10	2 × 10	2 × 10
	2 × 10	2 × 10	2 × 10	2 × 10	2 × 10	2 × 10

Thursday	Week 1	Week 2	Week 3	Week 4	Week 5	Week 6
	2 × 5	2 × 5	2 × 5	2 × 5	2 × 5	2 × 5
	2 × 10	2 × 10	2 × 10	2 × 10	2 × 10	2 × 10
	2 × 5	2 × 5	2 × 5	2 × 5	2 × 5	2 × 5
	2 × 5	2 × 5	2 × 5	2 × 5	2 × 5	2 × 5
	2 × 5	2 × 5	2 × 5	2 × 5	2 × 5	2 × 5
	2 × 10	2 × 10	2 × 10	2 × 10	2 × 10	2 × 10
	2 × 10	2 × 10	2 × 10	2 × 10	2 × 10	2 × 10
	2 × 10	2 × 10	2 × 10	2 × 10	2 × 10	2 × 10

Comments

Date

Sample Flexibility Card

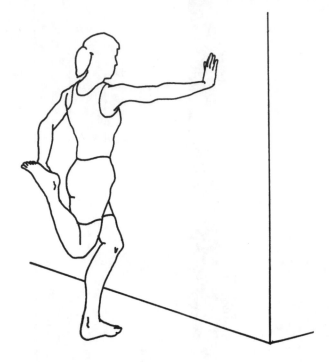

Quadriceps Stretch

Muscles stretched: quadriceps (thigh)

Sample Stretches

Feet and ankles

Lower legs

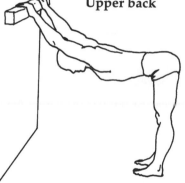

Adductors

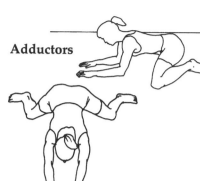

Quadriceps

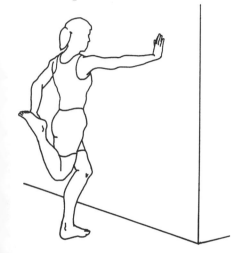

Hamstrings

Hips and gluteals

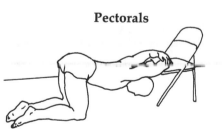

Lower torso

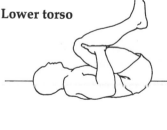

Pectorals

Upper back

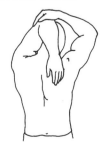

Shoulders

Neck

Arms and wrists

Alter, Michael J. 1998. *Sport Stretch* 2nd ed. Champaign, IL: Human Kinetics.

Estimated Energy Expenditures for Common Activities

Activity	Cal/min/lb	Cal/min/140 lb	Cal/10 min/lb
Badminton	0.214	29.9	2.14
Baseball (except pitching)	0.132	18.5	1.32
Basketball	0.304	42.6	3.04
Billiards	0.095	13.3	0.95
Bowling	0.207	29.0	2.07
Canoeing (leisurely pace)	0.099	13.9	0.99
Card playing	0.055	7.7	0.55
Carpet sweeping	0.101	14.2	1.01
Circuit training	0.408	57.1	4.08
Cooking	0.101	14.2	1.01
Cycling, 5.5 mph (11:00/mile)	0.141	19.7	1.41
Cycling, 9.4 mph (6:25/mile)	0.220	30.9	2.20
Dancing, aerobic (moderate)	0.225	31.5	2.25
Dancing, modern	0.159	22.2	1.59
Eating	0.051	7.1	0.51
Field hockey	0.304	42.6	3.04
Fishing	0.141	19.7	1.41
Food shopping	0.132	18.5	1.32
Football	0.291	40.7	2.91
Frisbee	0.220	30.9	2.20
Gardening	0.198	27.8	1.98
Grass mowing	0.247	34.6	2.47
Golf	0.187	26.2	1.87
Ice hockey	0.346	48.4	3.46
Jogging, 5.3 mph (11:30/mile)	0.298	41.7	2.98
Jogging, 6.7 mph (9:00/mile)	0.425	59.6	4.25
Jogging, 7.5 mph (8:00/mile)	0.461	64.5	4.61
Judo	0.432	60.5	4.32
Jumping rope, 70/min	0.357	50.0	3.57
Jumping rope, 125/min	0.390	54.6	3.90
Jumping rope, 145/min	0.436	61.1	4.36
Karate	0.445	62.3	4.45
Lacrosse	0.328	46.0	3.28
Lying at ease	0.048	6.8	0.48
Mopping	0.132	18.5	1.32
Sitting quietly	0.046	6.5	0.46
Standing quietly	0.057	8.0	0.57
Tennis	0.240	33.6	2.40
Walking, normal pace	0.176	24.7	1.76
Writing (sitting)	0.064	8.9	0.64

More About Physical Best, the Program, and the American Fitness Alliance

Physical Best is the educational component of a comprehensive health-related physical education program. It's designed to support existing curriculums and enable teachers to help students meet NASPE's health-related fitness standards. Physical Best resources include:

- *Physical Best Activity Guide—Elementary Level*
- *Physical Best Activity Guide—Secondary Level*
- The teacher's guide, *Physical Education for Lifelong Fitness*
- Educational workshops available through AAHPERD, which enable teachers to become certified as Physical Best Health-Fitness Specialists, call 1-800-213-7193, extension 426

The Physical Best program is offered through The American Fitness Alliance (AFA), a collaborative effort of AAHPERD, the Cooper Institute for Aerobics Research (CIAR), and Human Kinetics. AFA also offers assessment resources, which can be combined with Physical Best to create a complete health-related physical education program:

- The *FITNESSGRAM* test for evaluating students' physical fitness, developed by CIAR
- *The Brockport Physical Fitness Test*, a national test developed specifically for youths with disabilities
- *FitSmart*, the first national test designed to assess high school students' knowledge of concepts and principles of physical fitness

Additional AFA support resources are available and even more are in development, such as a physical activity text for high school students and a middle school version of FitSmart. All AFA resources are designed to foster the development of quality health-related physical education programs that promote the benefits of lifelong physical activity and health in young people.

Sponsorship for Physical Best is provided by Gopher Sport and Mars, Incorporated.